Air Fryer Cookbook

The Complete Air Fryer Cookbook – Delicious and Simple Recipes For Your Air Fryer

Table of Contents

Section I: Welcome to the World of Air fryers!

Introduction

Did you know that you can lose weight, get healthy, clean up your diet, save dollars and still enjoy mouth-watering, indulgent, utterly delicious foods?
Sounds too good to be true doesn't it? Sounds like something you'd hear in an infomercial or like something a dishonest salesman would tell you.
But you'll be surprised to know that it's absolutely 100% true.
You just need to learn the art of air frying!

What's an Air Fryer?

An air fryer is a brilliant kitchen appliance that 'fries' your food by pushing super-hot air around your food. You get the same crunchy texture you enjoy with traditional fried foods, but with a fraction of the calories. You can either use the air fryer exactly as it is or spray a small amount of oil inside the air fryer to create an even crunchier exterior. Yum!

What's even better is that you don't have to only cook foods you'd traditionally fry like French fries and fried chicken, but you can also roast, bake and grill with ease. Many models provide great accessories that help you do this, or you can simply use your own, provided they fit! This makes it the perfect all-round kitchen device. Most models are also 100% dishwasher-safe so you can avoid all the nasty mess that usually comes when you cook fried food at home.

You're probably asking yourself if the food tastes any good, because that's the exact same question I asked before I got my hands on an air fryer. And the answer is YES! The moment I had my first bite of food from the air fryer, I was hooked! I couldn't believe that healthy food tasted so good.

How do you use an air fryer?

It's difficult to explain how to use your air fryer when I'm not there next to you and you might not have the same model as I use.

Having said that, air fryers generally come with four parts which I *can* definitely explain to you here. You have an egg-shaped oven which is comprised of the outside, the wire basket and the rack. Most of the time, the food goes into the basket, otherwise it goes into the cooking accessory you're using for that particular recipe.

Note that there isn't a place to put any oil- simply spray the inside with oil as you start cooking or use a drop of oil with the ingredients themselves. Throughout this recipe, I'll let you know what you need to do to get the most from your recipe.

Cooking times usually work out similar to those you'd need if you were using a traditional cooking method, but feel free to experiment to get the best results for you. Again, I've included cooking times with all the recipes in this book.

What to expect in this book

I've written this book because I want you to see just how amazing air fryers are, and help you learn to use it to create delicious, healthy meals for yourself, your family, your friends and anyone else who might want to sample your amazing cooking.

To get you started, I've gathered together a massive 101 recipes that cover everything from appetizers, side dishes, meat, fish, seafood, poultry, cakes and deserts and even dedicated a whole section for anyone out the following a vegan, vegetarian or plant-based diet.

As far as possible, I've kept the ingredients list short and the steps brief to keep things nice and easy for you. Having said that, you will find several recipes with a longer list of ingredients and steps, so you can experience just how versatile your air fryer can be, and how exquisite the food that comes out of it can be. I'd recommend you stick with the shorter recipes at first then branch out as your skills grow.

So, let's not stay here talking. Let's dive right into section II- the recipes! Enjoy!

Section II: Air Fryer Recipes

Breakfasts

Sausage and Tomato Frittata

If you're looking for a fast but utterly delicious breakfast that contains plenty of blood-sugar friendly protein and tons of taste, you're going to adore this tasty breakfast. Awesome served with plenty of Tabasco sauce.

Serves: 1

Ingredients:
- 1 tbsp olive oil
- 4 cherry tomatoes, halved
- ½ Italian sausage
- 3 free-range eggs
- Chopped fresh parsley
- Parmesan cheese, grated
- Salt and pepper, to taste

Method:
1. Firstly, turn on your air fryer and turn the heat to 360 °F/ 180°C.
2. Next place the baking accessory onto the counter, pour and heat up the olive oil, and place the cherry tomatoes and sausage inside. Place into the air fryer and cook for five minutes.
3. Meanwhile, take a small bowl and whisk together the rest of the ingredients. Pour this over the tomatoes and sausage, spreading evenly. Cook for a further 5 minutes.
4. Serve and enjoy!

The Ultimate Fried English Breakfast

There's nothing like an English breakfast to get you fueled and ready for anything life can throw at you. This revamped air fryer version skips the unhealthy fats but keeps 100% of the flavor and 110% of the taste. Enjoy!

Serves: 4

Ingredients:
- 8 medium sausages
- 8 rashers un-smoked back bacon
- 1 can baked beans
- 4 free-range eggs
- 8 slices toast, buttered

Method:
1. Firstly, turn on your air fryer and turn the heat to 320 °F/ 160°C, then place the sausages and bacon inside. Cook for 10 minutes. If cooked through, remove and place to one side or if you think they need longer, pop to one side inside your air fryer.
2. Turn the heat up to 390 °F/ 200°C.
3. Take two ramekins and place the baked beans into one, and the egg into the other.
4. Add the ramekins containing the beans and egg, then cook for a further 10 minutes until it all looks lovely.
5. Serve with plenty of hot buttered toast and enjoy!

Mouth-Watering French Toast Sticks

Since my childhood visits to my grandmother's house, I've been totally in love with the gently spiced, warming flavor of French toast. The only problem is, the regular version is loaded with unhealthy fats and calories, and isn't something you'd want to be eating every day. That's why I was sooo pleased when I realized I could do exactly the same recipe but in my beloved air fryer. Now I can eat it guilt-free almost every day if I want to. You can also serve the French toast in bigger slices.

Serves: 2

Ingredients:
- 2 free-range eggs, beaten
- Pinch of salt, to taste
- 1 tsp ground cinnamon
- ¼ ground nutmeg
- Pinch ground cloves
- 4 generous slices of your favorite kind of bread
- 2 tbsp butter, softened
- Maple syrup to serve
- Cooking spray

Method:
1. Firstly, turn on your air fryer and turn the heat to 350 °F/ 180°C.
2. Take a large bowl and mix together all the ingredients except the maple syrup and the maple syrup. Stir well to combine.
3. Next butter the bread on both sides and cut into strips of whatever size you like.
4. Dip each of the strips into the egg mixture and place into the air fryer. Don't worry if they won't all fit- you'll probably have to cook them in two batches.
5. Cook for two minutes, then open up and spray with oil, then turn them over and cook for a further four minutes.
6. Serve and enjoy with the maple syrup, and a nice dollop of cream or Greek yogurt if you like to add. Yummy!

Chili Breakfast Soufflé

Impress your friends and family with this light and flurry soufflé, which will melt in your mouth whilst the gentle chili flavor spreads throughout your mouth. Ready in less than 10 minutes, you can whip them up, head to the shower and have them ready fast. They make an awesome brunch for the whole family (although you might want to skip the chili if there are kids around).

Serves: 4

Ingredients
- 4 free-range eggs
- 4 tbsp light cream
- Fresh parsley, chopped
- Large pinch red chili pepper
- Salt and pepper, to taste

Method
1. Firstly, turn on your air fryer and turn the heat to 390 °F/ 200°C.
2. Next, grab a big bowl, add the eggs and stir through the cream. Add in the parsley, chili, salt and pepper and stir well to combine.
3. Take your ramekin dishes and fill them halfway up with the egg mixture then place them into the air fryer and cook for 8 minutes.
4. Serve and enjoy!

Easy Onion and Cheese Omelet

I think I'm slightly addicted to the flavor of cheese and onion, and you will be too when you sink your teeth into this fluffy, incredibly filling omelet. It tastes even better when served with generous hunks of freshly buttered toast and makes the perfect mid-week breakfast. Enjoy!

Serves: 2

Ingredients:
- 4 free-range eggs
- Pepper, to taste
- Soy Sauce, to taste
- Cooking Spray
- 1-2 medium onion, sliced
- Cheddar Cheese (grated)

Method:
1. Take medium bowl, crack the eggs into it and whisk well until they're completely combined. Add your seasonings such as soy sauce and pepper and then place to one side.
2. Turning your attention to your air fryer, spray cooking oil inside the pan then place the onions inside and fry for around 10 minutes at 350°F/ 180°C.
3. Next open up the air fryer and add the egg mixture, followed by the cheese then pop back inside until the eggs are cooked to perfection.
4. Serve and enjoy.

(*Note: you can omit the onions if you're short on time, or replace with onion powder if you'd prefer.*)

Turkey and Avocado Breakfast Burrito

Burritos make an absolutely brilliant breakfast because you can just throw anything you want to inside, wrap it up, and tuck right in. This delicious recipe takes turkey, avocado, pepper, eggs, cheese and mouth-watering salsa to make something incredible.

Serves: 2

Ingredients:
- 4 free-range eggs
- Salt & pepper, to taste
- 2 x tortillas
- 6-8 slices turkey or chicken breast, cooked
- ½ red bell pepper, sliced
- ½ avocado, sliced
- ¼ cup (25g) mozzarella cheese, grated
- 4 tbsp salsa
- Cooking spray

Method:
1. Take a medium bowl, break the eggs into it and whisk well until combined. Then add a pinch of salt and pepper.
2. Open your air fryer, spray the inside of the tray with cooking spray and pour in the egg mixture. Cook for 5 minutes at 390°F/ 200°C, then scrape into a clean bowl.
3. Now let's start building your burritos. Split the eggs between the two tortillas, followed by the turkey (or chicken), the pepper, the avocado, the cheese and the salsa. Roll it up carefully.
4. Spray the inside of the air fryer again and place the burritos inside. Cook at 350°F/180°C for 3-5 minutes until your burrito is perfectly toasted.
5. Serve and enjoy.

Gouda, Tomato and Onion Breakfast Pie

If you haven't tasted the nutty, buttery taste of gouda for breakfast, you really haven't lived! Teamed with the gently bite of onions, tomatoes and soft eggs, it makes the perfect crust-less quiche for the perfect weekend brunch. Just wait 'til they start begging you for the recipe!!

Serves: 2-4

Ingredients:

- 4 free-range eggs
- ½ cup (180ml) milk
- 1 cup (125g) shredded gouda cheese
- ½ cup (100g) diced tomatoes
- 4 tbsp diced onion
- Salt and pepper, to taste

Method:

1. Easy! Just grab a large ramekin (but make sure it fits inside your air fryer) and place all the ingredients inside. If not, halve the quantities and spread between two batches. Stir well to combine.
2. Place into the air fryer and cook for 30 minutes at 340°F/170°C.
3. Serve and enjoy!

Pecan Rolled Oat Granola

Who'd have thought you could make nutty, scrummy granola in your air fryer? Not me! But it turns out that it's ultra-delicious, fast, hands-off and totally amazing. Serve with a big dollop of fat-free yogurt or sprinkle over ice-cream for the most amazing taste EVER.

Serves: as many people as you allow!

Ingredients:
- 1 ½ cups (135g) rolled oats
- ½ cup (60g) pecans, roughly chopped
- Pinch salt
- 2-3 tbsp honey
- 2 tbsp butter, melted
- ½ cup (75g) sunflower seeds
- ½ cup (75g) raisins
- Cooking spray

Method:
1. Grab a nice big bowl and place the oats, seeds, pecans, and that pinch of salt inside. Stir well to combine.
2. Using a small bowl, combine the honey and melted butter, stir well and then pour into the oat mixture.
3. Spray the inside of your air fryer with cooking spray and cook the oat mixture for 5 minutes on 350°F/180°C. Open up and stir well halfway through. Depending on the size of your air fryer, you might want to do this in batches.
4. Remove it from the air fryer and pour into a bowl to cool. Add sunflower seeds and raisins and stir well.
5. Eat immediately or store in an airtight container.

Scrambled Eggs with Cheese and Tomato

If you've never tried scrambled eggs in your air fryer before, you'll be astonished at how tasty this recipe is! Think soft, fluffy and the perfect way to start the day. Just make them and you'll understand...

Serves: 2

Ingredients:

- 4 free-range eggs
- ¾ cup (200ml) milk
- Salt and pepper, to taste
- ½ cup (55g) cheddar cheese, grated
- 8 cherry tomatoes, halved
- Cooking spray

Method:

1. Start by breaking the eggs into a large bowl or jug, adding the milk, adding the seasoning and then giving it all a nice whisk to combine.
2. Open up your air fryer and spray with cooking oil.
3. Then add the egg mixture to the pan and cook for 6 minutes on 350°C/ 180°C.
4. Open, scrape down the eggs, add the tomatoes and give it a nice stir, before cooking again for a further 3 minutes.
5. Serve sprinkled with the grated cheese and enjoy!

Air Fryer Tofu Scramble

Just because you're vegetarian or vegan, doesn't mean that you can't enjoy an awesome cooked breakfast to start the day. Try this soft tofu and potato scramble and you'll think you've died and gone to veggie heaven!

Serves: 2-4

Ingredients:
- 1 block tofu, cut into 1" (2.5cm) pieces
- 2 tbsp olive oil (1 + 1 tbsp)
- 1 tsp turmeric
- ½ tsp garlic powder
- ½ tsp onion powder
- 2 tbsp soy sauce
- 2-3 potatoes, chopped into small pieces
- ½ cup (75g) chopped onion
- 4 cups (300g) broccoli florets

Method:
1. Firstly, take a large bowl and add to it the drained tofu, 1 tsp of olive oil, turmeric, garlic powder, onion powder and onion. Lastly add the soy sauce and stir well so that the juices cover the tofu completely.
2. Meanwhile, take another bowl and add the potatoes and onion, followed by the remaining olive and then pop them into the air fryer for about 15 minutes at 400°F/ 200°C. Take them out and give them a good stir halfway through the cooking time.
3. Open up the air fryer, then add the tofu plus any juices. Turn the temperature down to 370°F/ 190°C and cook for another 15 minutes.
4. Meanwhile, place the broccoli into a bowl, add some soy sauce, give it a toss and add to the air fryer around 5 minutes before the end.
5. Serve and enjoy!

Air Fryer Vegan Breakfast Casserole

I love breakfast casseroles because they're a super-easy way to eat hot, filling, nourishing food without having to spend hours slaving away in the kitchen. This vegan tofu-based version with mushrooms, garlic and a touch of my favorite-chili- promises to be a breakfast you'll never forget. I doubt they'll believe it's vegan either!

Serves: 2

Ingredients:
- 1 tsp olive oil
- 1 small onion, diced
- 1 large carrot, diced
- 2 small celery stalks, diced
- ½ cup (90g) bell pepper, diced
- 1 tsp minced garlic
- ½ cup (70g) shiitake mushrooms, diced
- Salt and pepper, to taste
- ½ tsp dried dill
- ½ tsp red pepper flakes
- ½ tsp ground cumin
- 1 tsp dried oregano
- 7 oz. (200g) extra-firm tofu
- 2 tbsp nutritional yeast (optional)
- 2 tbsp plain soy yogurt
- 2 tbsp water
- 1 tbsp lemon juice
- ½ cup (90g) cooked quinoa
- Cooking oil

Method:
1. We'll need to start this one on the stove top. Heat the olive oil in a skillet, add the onion and carrots and gently cook for 5 minutes until they start to soften. Next add the celery, pepper and garlic and cook for a few more minutes.
2. Finally add the shiitake mushrooms, salt and pepper, dill, red pepper flakes, cumin and oregano and stir well. Cook until softened.
3. Meanwhile, blend the tofu, nutritional yeast, yogurt, water and lemon juice until creamy then add this to the skillet, along with the quinoa. Stir well to combine.
4. Finally, add this all to a greased air fryer pan and cook for 15-20 minutes on 350°F/180°C.
5. Leave to rest for five minutes before serving.

Vegan Hash Browns

Hands up if you LOVE hash browns...yep me too. But it's another one of those breakfast options which is usually high-fat, high-calorie and definitely off the menu. Hail the mighty air fryer! Simply follow this recipe, cook it up in your air fryer and you'll be amazed!

Serves: 8 pieces (so serves as many as you like!)

Ingredients:
- 4 large potatoes, peeled and shredded
- 2 tsp olive oil (1 + 1 tsp)
- 2 tbsp corn flour
- Salt and pepper to taste
- 2 tsp chili flakes (optional)
- 1 tsp garlic powder (optional)
- 1 tsp onion powder (optional)
- Cooking spray

Method:
1. Put the potatoes into a large bowl of cold water and leave to soak for a minute or two. Drain and repeat. This will drain excess starch and make those hash browns even yummier!
2. Place a teaspoon of the olive oil in a skillet and cook the shredded potatoes for 3-4 minutes until soft. Place onto a clean plate and allow it to cool.
3. Take a large bowl and add the potatoes, the corn flour, the salt and pepper and any spices you're using then mix well until it combines well.
4. Place it into the fridge for 20 minutes to firm.
5. Preheat your air fryer to 350°F/180°C and turn your attention to the hash browns. Take them from the fridge and cut into whatever size pieces you desire.
6. Spray the wire basket of your air fryer with some oil, add the pieces of hash brown and fry for 15 minutes. Flip them halfway through cooking to help them cook all over.
7. Serve and enjoy!

Appetizers & Side Dishes

Crispy Paprika Potato Wedges

Oh wow, I can't tell you just how good these spicy potato wedges taste with a large juicy burger, buried in a huge pile of melted cheese or just eaten straight from the air fryer. You'll just have to try them for yourself!

Serves: 6

Ingredients:
- 6 medium russet potatoes
- 2 tbsp oil
- 1 ½ tsp paprika
- ½ tsp salt
- ½ tsp black pepper

Method:
1. Start by preparing your potatoes! Give them a wash under running water and chop off any dark pieces or knots.
2. Meanwhile, fill a large pan with water and bring to the boil. Throw in the potatoes and cook until tender. (This might take 30-45 minutes as they are so big.)
3. Transfer the potatoes to the fridge once cooked so they can cool off.
4. Place the oil, paprika, salt and pepper into a bowl and mix well until combined.
5. Take the potatoes from the fridge and cut into wedges, then place into the bowl of spices and mix well until everything is nicely coated.
6. Transfer this to your air fryer and cook on 390°F/ 200°C for 15 minutes, turning often.
7. Serve and enjoy!

Authentic Spanish Patatas Bravas with Vegan Avocado Aioli

One of the best things about visiting Barcelona in Spain is heading to a tapas bar and filling up on small bite-sized portions of mouth-watering foods. Whenever I'm lucky enough to go, I always order plenty! But I do have to say that thanks to the astonishingly good avocado aioli, this healthy version comes a very close second.

Serves: 4

Ingredients:

For the Patatas Bravas:
- 6 medium potatoes, peeled and cubed
- Salt, to taste
- 1 tsp smoked paprika
- 2 tsp olive oil
- 4 tbsp hot chili sauce
- Chopped flat-leaf parsley, to garnish

For the avocado aioli:
- 2 small avocados, pitted and chopped
- 1 garlic clove, chopped
- Juice of one lemon
- ¼ tsp salt

Method:
1. Preheat the air fryer to 290°F/150°C then turn your attention to making those patatas bravas.
2. Place the potatoes into a large bowl with the salt, paprika and olive oil.
3. Open up your air fryer, place the potatoes into the wire basket and cook for 25-30 minutes until brown.
4. Meanwhile, for the avocado aioli, take a food processor and add all the aioli ingredients. Blend until smooth then cover and pop into the fridge until the potatoes are cooked.
5. Then place a tablespoon of the chili sauce onto each plate, followed by approximately a cup of the potatoes. Top with the avocado aioli and parsley, serve and enjoy!

Korean Bang Bang Broccoli

Imagine broccoli fried in a light batter and then drizzled with a sauce that is spicy, nutty and sweet. Popular in Korean and China, this fried snack will make your mouth water.

Serves: 4

Ingredients:

For the sauce:
- 4 tbsp mayonnaise
- 2 tbsp chili paste
- 1 tbsp honey or maple syrup

For the batter:
- 1 cup (235ml) milk
- 1 tsp apple cider vinegar
- ¾ cup (90g) flour
- ½ cup (60g) cornstarch
- 1 tsp salt
- 2 tsp hot sauce

For the broccoli:
- 2 cups (100g) panko bread crumbs (can substitute with regular breadcrumbs)
- 1 head broccoli
- Oil for frying
- Chives for garnish (optional)

Method:
1. For the sauce, in a small bowl, add the mayonnaise, the chili paste and your choice or sweetener. Give it all a nice stir to combine then put into the fridge whilst you make the rest.
2. Take a medium bowl and add the milk with the apple cider vinegar. Leave to rest for a few minutes.
3. In a separate bowl, add the flour, cornstarch and salt and stir well to combine. Then add the hot sauce and milk mixture then whisk well until completely lump-free.
4. Place the panko into another bowl, and take out the sauce from the fridge.
5. Preheat the air fryer to 400°F/200°C.
6. Cut the broccoli into florets and dip into the batter, then the breadcrumbs and pop into the air fryer. Cook for 15 minutes until crispy.
7. Serve with the sauce and enjoy!

"WOW!" Brussels Sprouts

Yes, that's a massive claim, but I promise that you really will go 'wow' then you try these beauties. In fact, you'll never believe that they're made from the same little green bullet that makes kids and adults frown.

Serves: 4-6

Ingredients:
- 1 lb. (450g) Brussels Sprouts
- 3 tbsp olive oil
- 3 tsp salt

Method:
1. Nice and easy! Cut off the stems and remove any brown or lose leaves from the sprouts. Cut in halve then give them a wash.
2. Pop into a large bowl with the olive and salt and give them a nice stir to combine well.
3. Turn your air fryer onto 375°F/ 190°C, pop the sprouts into the wire basket and cook for 15 minutes. Check often and turn when required.
4. Serve and enjoy!

Homemade Potato Chips

I don't mind admitting that I'm a happy potato chip addict these days, thanks to my air fryer. I just need a potato or two and I can make a TON of potato chips to keep me nibbling all night long. These are fresher than the store-bought kind and (shhh...) actually quite good for you.

Serves: however many hungry people you're willing to share with!

Ingredients:
- 2 medium potatoes, washed
- ½ tsp olive oil
- Salt, to taste

Method:
1. Wash your potatoes, and peel them if you want to. Then slice them as thinly as you can with a mandolin. You can also use a knife for this, but it can be more challenging.
2. Now place the potato slices into a bowl of cool water and leave to rest for 30 minutes to remove some of the starch.
3. Remove the slices from the water and gently dry.
4. Place them into a large bowl with olive oil and salt and toss well to cover.
5. Now turn on the air fryer, turn the heat on 400°F/200°C and cook the potato chips in the basket for 15-20 minutes until cooked.

Vegetable Spring Rolls Recipe

This delicious Asian-inspired spring rolls make the perfect appetizer, light snack or side dish for the whole family. Packed with delicious crunch, a whole lot of nutrients and none of the calories, they make a brilliant dish you'll want to make again…and again…and again.

Serves: 8

Ingredients:
For the filling:
- 2 cups (780g) shredded cabbage
- 1 large carrot, grated
- 1 onion, sliced
- ½ bell pepper, sliced
- 2" (5cm) piece fresh ginger
- 8 cloves garlic
- 2 tbsp cooking oil
- Pinch sugar
- Salt, to taste
- 1 tsp soy sauce
- 1 tbsp ground pepper
- Spring onion, to garnish

For the wrap:
- 10 sheets spring roll sheet
- 2 tbsp corn flour
- Water, as needed

Method:
1. Usually the spring roll sheets come frozen, so make sure you've taken yours out to defrost at least 1 hour before cooking.
2. We'll start by preparing the filling. Take a large bowl, add the shredded cabbage, carrot, onion and bell pepper and given them a nice stir to combine. Follow this with the ginger and the garlic and stir again.
3. Pop a wok over a high heat; add the oil, the vegetables and some salt and sugar. Then cook gently for just 2-3 minutes. Remove from the heat.
4. Stir through the soy sauce and pepper and set to one side.
5. Take another bowl and add the cornflower and a small amount of water.

6. Let's start rolling! Take a sheet of the wrap and cut it into the size you want- two pieces are good for large spring rolls and four are good for small spring rolls.
7. Now place a small amount of stuffing into one corner, then roll tightly, tucking in the sides are you go. Seal the roll using the corn flour paste, then repeat with the remaining filling.
8. Preheat your air fryer to 350°F/ 180°C then place the sheets into the wire basket. Cook for 20 minutes, flipping half way through to cook evenly.
9. Serve and enjoy!

Salmon Croquettes

You can guarantee that if I whip up a batch of these melt-in-the-mouth salmon croquettes, they'll be gone faster than you can say 'I love my air fryer'! They have that perfect crunch which gives way to tender, fragrant salmon, they're rich in healthy omega 3 oils and they're really easy to make. Try them!

Serves: 4 (makes 16 croquettes)

Ingredients:
- 14 oz. (425g) tinned red salmon, drained
- 2 free range eggs
- Pinch of herbs
- Salt and pepper, to taste
- 2 tbsp spring onions, chopped
- 1 cup (100g) breadcrumbs (adjust as needed)
- 5 tbsp vegetable oil

Method:
1. Start by opening the tin of salmon, draining it and carefully removing any bones. Place into a bowl and mash well.
2. Break in the egg, add the herbs, salt and pepper and the spring onions. Mix well.
3. In a separate bowl, mix together the breadcrumbs and oil until combined.
4. Take a spoon of the salmon mixture and shape into a croquette shape in your hand, then roll into the crumbs and place into your air fryer basket. Repeat with the remaining mixture.
5. Place into your air fryer and cook at 390°F/200°C for 7-10 minutes, until golden.
6. Serve and enjoy!

Air Fryer Seasoned French Fries

Everyone loves fries, right? But we often resist because they're just not good for our waistlines nor our cholesterol levels. But again, we can indulge time and time again because these little beauties are relatively healthy! Yay! Your kids will love them, your partner's eye will glisten in excitement when they land on the table and your buddies will make sure not a single fry lies uneaten!

Serves: approximately 4

Ingredients:
- 4 medium potatoes
- 2 tbsp olive oil
- 1 tbsp seasoned salt (regular salt works fine too)

Method:
1. Get started by washing those potatoes really well and slicing into fries.
2. Put them into a bowl of cool water and leave for 30 minutes to get rid of the excess starch.
3. Drain and dry with a clean tea towel then place into a large bowl.
4. Add the olive oil and seasoned salt and then mix well. You can also use regular salt and your choice of spices at this point if you'd prefer.
5. Place into your air fryer and cook at 400°F/ 200°C for around 15 minutes.
6. Serve and enjoy!

Cauliflower Buffalo Bites

This cauliflower recipe is yet another place where your air fryer will really shine. It takes humble cauli and gives it such a facelift that it's hard to believe it's actually a veg. Suitable for vegetarians, vegans and vegetable-haters alike, it's spicy, garlicky and simply YUM!

Serves: 6

Ingredients:
- 1 large head cauliflower, cut into bite-size florets
- Olive oil to drizzle
- 2 tsp garlic powder
- ¼ tsp salt
- 1/8 tsp pepper

Method:
1. This one is super-easy. Simply place the cauliflower florets into a large bowl and drizzle a small amount of olive oil until just coated.
2. Next add the garlic powder, salt and pepper and mix together well.
3. Now pop this into the wire basket of your air fryer and cook on 400°F/ 200°C for around 15 minutes. Make sure you check and turn as required.
4. Serve and enjoy! (These taste amazing with blue cheese dressing, hummus or garlic mayo.)

Cajun Spiced Snack Mix

If you're getting ready for the Superbowl, or Thanksgiving or you're having another gathering but you don't want to buy premade snack mix, just grab some ingredients and make this one. It's incredibly easy to make, inexpensive and also very moreish. Just watch how much spice you use- your mouth might soon be one fire!

Serves: 10 cups

Ingredients:
For the Cajun Seasoning:
- 2 tsp salt
- 1 tsp cayenne pepper
- 1 tsp garlic
- 1 tsp paprika
- ½ tsp oregano
- ½ tsp thyme
- ½ tsp onion powder
- 1 tsp black pepper
- ½ cup (110g) butter or coconut oil, melted

For the mix:
- 2 cups (30g approx..) mini wheat thin crackers
- 2 cups (125g) peanuts
- 2 cups (160g) mini pretzels
- 4 cups (32g) plain popcorn

Method:
1. For Cajun seasoning, simply place all the spices into a bowl and stir well to combine. Add the melted butter, stir well and set to one side.
2. Now grab yourself another bowl and combine the crackers, peanuts, pretzels and popcorn. Pour the melted butter mixture over the snack mix and mix well.
3. Place into your air fryer and cook for around 10 minutes on 370°F/190°C until toasted.

Beer Battered Onion Rings

I love the way that the air fryer lets you keep eating your favorite foods even those ones that are usually high fat, high calorie and harmful for your health. The addition of beer makes them light, melt-in-the-mouth and full of flavor.

Serves: 2-4

Ingredients:
- ⅔ cup (80g) flour
- ½ tsp baking soda
- 1 tsp paprika
- 1 tsp salt
- ½ tsp freshly ground black pepper
- ¾ cup (180ml) beer
- 1 free-range egg, beaten
- 1 ½ cups (135g) fine breadcrumbs
- 1 large onion, peeled and sliced into ½-inch rings
- Cooking spray

Method:
1. Firstly, take a bowl and mix together the flour, baking soda, paprika, salt and pepper. Then add the beer and the egg and give it a nice mix until lump-free and completely combined.
2. Take a separate dish and pour the breadcrumbs onto it.
3. Dip the onion rings into the batter with the help of a fork, then into the breadcrumbs and put it aside. Repeat with the rest of the sliced onion rings.
4. Once they are all nicely coated, give them a quick spray with some cooking oil and place into the wire basket of your air fryer. Cook for 15 minutes at 360°F/180°C, checking them about halfway through to make sure they're evenly cooked.
5. Serve and enjoy!

Spicy Buffalo Wings

Mmmm... Buffalo wings are probably the best thing ever invented for hungry tummies and spicy-food lovers. Using just a handful of ingredients, these will be ready in no time so you can satisfy your cravings pronto.

Serves: 4

Ingredients:
For the wings...
- 2lb (900g) chicken wings
- 3 tbsp butter, melted
- 4 tbsp hot sauce
- Salt, to taste (optional)

For the finishing sauce...
- 3 tbsp butter, melted
- 4 tbsp hot sauce

Method:
1. Firstly for the chicken wings, cut off the wing tips then split the drums from the wings and place both into a large bowl.
2. Mix the melted butter hot sauce and mix well to blend. Pour this over the wings and leave them to marinate for as long as you can.
   (If you've got plenty of time, you can leave them for a couple of hours or overnight for best results.)
3. Once they are ready to cook, throw the chicken into your Air Fryer and cook on 400°F/ 200°C for 15 minutes. Don't forget to turn them about half way through to make sure they cook evenly.
4. Meanwhile, combine the rest of the butter with the hot sauce and stirring well.
5. When your wings are cooked, pour the sauce over the top then serve and enjoy!

Easy Baked Garlic Parsley Potatoes

Potatoes are AMAZING in an air fryer! They're so crispy and so easy that it's tempting to just make them for every meal or snack. You'll see what I mean when you taste them.
Serves: 2

Ingredients:
- 3 large baking potatoes
- 1 tbsp olive oil
- 1 tbsp salt
- 1 tbsp dried garlic
- 1 tsp parsley
- Sour cream, chives, or any of your favorite accompaniment

Method:
1. Give the potatoes a good wash, then prick them with a fork to allow the steam to escape (if you skip this part, they may explode!)
2. Place the potatoes into a large bowl and cover with the oil and seasonings. Rub well to make sure they're well covered.
3. Place them into the wire basket of your air fryer and cook for 30-45 minutes at 390°F/200°C.
4. Serve and enjoy with sour cream and chives, or your favorite accompaniment.

Homemade Corn Tortilla Chips

Yep, you can make these babies at home. Here's how.

Serves: 1-2

Ingredients:
- 8 corn tortillas
- 1 tbsp olive oil
- Salt, to taste

Method:
1. Firstly, place the corn tortillas onto a chopping board and cut into triangles.
2. Brush with olive oil and then place into the wire basket of your air fryer.
3. Cook on 390°F/200°C for 3-5 minutes until crispy.
4. Remove from the air fryer, sprinkle with salt and tuck in!

Garlic and Herb Roasted Chickpeas

When my sister was pregnant, she always used to turn up at my apartment eating. According to her, it was to keep the baby strong, but I knew what was really going on. Secretly, she had a thing for roasted chickpeas and was using it as an excuse. But we don't need any excuses! So, let's make our own batch and enjoy them. Just keep them away from my sister!!

Serves: 4

Ingredients:
- 2 x 14 oz (2 x 450g) cans chickpeas
- 1 tbsp olive oil
- 1 tbsp nutritional yeast
- 2 tsp garlic powder
- 1 tbsp mixed herbs
- Sea salt and black pepper, to taste

Method:
1. Open up those cans of chickpeas and give them a good rinse under running water to get rid of all the gunk. Put them into a large bowl.
2. Add the olive oil followed by the seasonings and stir well to coat completely.
3. Pop into the wire basket of your air fryer and cook on 390°F/200°C for 15-20 minutes until perfectly crunchy. Don't forget to check them and turn midway through cooking to ensure they cook evenly.
4. Serve and enjoy!

Spinach & Sausage Stuffed Mushrooms

How about something a little bit different for your snack or appetizer? These cute little mushrooms are perfectly bite-sized, easy to create and full to the brim with well-rounded flavor.

Serves: 4-6

Ingredients:
- 7 button mushrooms, cleaned, stems removed and set aside
- Olive oil
- ½ cup cream cheese, softened
- 1 tbsp mayonnaise
- 10 leaves baby spinach, chopped finely
- 4 tsp Parmesan cheese, grated
- ¼ tsp black pepper
- 1/8 tsp salt
- A few drops of Tabasco sauce

Method:
1. Brush the mushrooms with a light coating of olive oil, then put aside.
2. Grab a large bowl and add the cream cheese and mayonnaise. Mix together well and set to one side.
3. Meanwhile, finely chop the mushroom stems and the spinach and add to your cream cheese mix. Stir well to combine, then season with salt and pepper, and add as much Tabasco sauce as you like and stir again.
4. Take a small spoonful of the mixture and pop into each mushroom cap and then sprinkle the Parmesan cheese over the top.
5. Place into the wire basket of your air fryer and cook for 12 minutes at 300°F/150°C.
6. Serve and enjoy!

Meat

Toad in the Hole

Toad in the Hole is a British dish made with sausages and the classic Yorkshire pudding, topped with a generous helping of gravy. If you've never tried it, you'll be surprised at how good it tastes. Of course, I like to skip the gravy and go with some US-style hot sauce, but don't tell the Brits!

Serves: 4

Ingredients:
- 1 cup (165g) flour
- 2 free-range eggs
- ¾ cup (160ml) milk
- ½ cup (120ml) cold water
- 1 red onion, finely sliced
- 1 clove garlic, finely chopped
- Salt and pepper, to taste
- 1 tbsp olive oil
- 8 small sausages
- 15 g rosemary sprigs

Method:
1. First, find a large dish that fits into your air fryer or use the one that the manufacturer provided. Whatever you opt for, make sure that it's heatproof!
2. Now get a large bowl and add the flour, followed by the eggs. Gently beat the eggs and then start slowly adding the milk, the water, the chopped onion and the garlic, followed by any salt and pepper. Mix well to combine.
3. Now place your sausages into the bottom of the pan and poke a small amount of rosemary into each one. Pour the batter you just made over the sausages then pop into the air fryer.
4. Cook on 320°F/160°C for 30 minutes until the batter has cooked through.
5. Serve and enjoy.

Sweet Sticky Pork Sausages

Whenever I'm in need of some proper comfort food, I open up my fridge and pull out everything I need to make these sticky sauces. Perfect when serves with potato mash or fries, they'll be ready within half an hour and on that table waiting for you. Mmmm…

Serves: 2-4

Ingredients:
- 3 tsp vegetable bouillon powder
- ¾ cup (170 ml) boiling water
- ½ cup (175g) caramelized onion chutney
- 2 tbsp balsamic vinegar
- 2 tbsp soft brown sugar
- 2 cups (300g) red onions, peeled and cut into chunks
- 8 butcher-style pork sausages

Method:
1. First, find a large dish that fits into your air fryer or use the one that the manufacturer provided. Whatever you opt for, make sure that it's heatproof!
2. Now for the sticky sauce, start by dissolving the bouillon powder in the boiling water then add the chutney, the vinegar, brown sugar, and the onions. Stir well to combine.
3. Finally, add the sausages to the mix and give it another stir. You want your sausages to be well coated.
4. Place this into the large dish you found earlier and cook in your air fryer for around 25-30 minutes on 180°C / 350°F. Don't forget to check and turn your sausages often to make sure they're cooking evenly.
5. Serve and enjoy!

Pumpkin and Pork Empanadas

These warming empanadas remind me of my grandmother's steaming meat pastries, don't ask me why! Lightly spiced and crunchy, you'll keep coming back for more once you've had your first bit. Just warning you!

Serves: 2-4 (makes 10 empanadas)

Ingredients:

- 2 tbsp olive oil
- ½ onion, diced
- 1 lb (450g) ground pork
- 1 ½ cups (330g) pumpkin purée
- 3 tbsp water
- 1 red chili pepper, minced
- ½ tsp cinnamon
- ½ tsp dried thyme
- 1 tsp salt
- Black pepper, to taste
- 1 package of 10 empanada discs (you can also use pastry dough)
- Olive oil

Method:

1. Start by warming a small amount of oil in a skillet and gently frying the onions and the pork for around 5 minutes.
2. Pour away the fat, then add the pumpkin, water, chili, cinnamon, thyme, salt and pepper and stir well to combine. Cook for 10 minutes to allow the flavors to really blend. Set this aside to cool.
3. Open up that packet of empanada discs and spread them out over your worktop. Add a couple of tablespoons of filling to each, brush the edges with water and then fold the dough towards the center, to form a Cornish pasty shape. Brush with olive oil and repeat with the rest.
4. Place the empanadas into the wire basket of your air fryer and cook on 370°F/180°C for around 15 minutes. Make sure you check often and turn as required.
5. Serve and enjoy!

Chinese-Style Beef & Broccoli

There's nothing like beef and broccoli to pick you up after a hard day's work. But sadly, if you go to a Chinese takeaway you're likely to eat something that is neither authentic nor healthy. Try this instead. It ticks all the right boxes and tastes awesome!

Serves: 4

Ingredients:
- 3 cups (750g) oyster sauce
- 2 tsp sesame oil
- 1 tsp cornstarch
- 1/3 cup (80ml) sherry
- 1 tsp soy sauce
- 1 tsp sugar
- ¾ lb (340g) steak, cut into strips
- 1 lb (450g) broccoli, cut into pieces
- 1 slice fresh ginger
- 1 clove garlic, minced
- 1 tbsp olive oil

Method:
1. For the marinade, take a medium bowl and pour into this the oyster sauce, sesame oil, cornstarch, sherry, soy sauce and sugar. Give it a nice stir until it's all well mixed.
2. Then place your steak strips into the sauce and leave for around an hour to marinade.
3. Remove from the marinade and place inside the wire basket of your air fryer, along with the broccoli, topped with the ginger, garlic and the olive oil.
4. Cook for 12 minutes on 390°F/200°C until cooked through.
5. Serve with noodles or rice and enjoy!

Roasted Beef-Stuffed Peppers

Stuffed peppers are a classic which I often forget all about, but as soon as I take a bite, I realize just how much I've been missing. Like a gorgeous beef chili in an edible package and topped with melty, tasty cheese, you'll keep coming back for more. This recipe is also really easy to double, triple or quadruple if you have a large crowd to feed.

Serves: 2

Ingredients:
- 2 medium green peppers, stems and seeds removed
- ½ medium onion, chopped
- 1 clove garlic, minced
- 1 tsp olive oil
- 8 oz (225g) lean ground beef
- ½ cup (120g) tomato sauce
- 1 tsp Worcestershire sauce
- ½ tsp salt
- ½ tsp black pepper
- 4 oz (110g) cheddar cheese, shredded

Method:
1. Start by preparing those peppers. Carefully slice off the top, to form a lid, then scoop out the seeds and pith inside. Bring a pan of water to boiling and quickly blanch the peppers for 3 minutes.
2. Now chop the onion and garlic and place into a skillet on stovetop with a small amount of olive oil. Cook until softened (takes around 5 minutes). Remove from the heat and allow it to cool slightly.
3. Take a large bowl and add the beef, cooked onion mixture, tomato sauce, Worcestershire, salt, pepper and half of the cheese. Stir well to combine.
4. Stuff this into your pre-prepared peppers and top with the remaining cheese.
5. Pop into the air fryer and cook for 15-20 minutes at 390°F/200°C until cooked through.
6. Serve and enjoy.

Homemade Steak & Ale Pie

My mother used to make the world's best steak and ale pie, so for the longest time, I'd avoid making my own. It would be too tricky, and it wouldn't taste the same, or so I thought. But I was wrong; this recipe tastes even better than my mom's. This one does take a bit of time to prep, but it's very much worth it!

Serves: 2

Ingredients:
- 1 tbsp olive oil
- 1 large onion, peeled and diced
- 1 lb (500g) beef stewing steak
- 1 tbsp tomato puree
- 1 can ale
- 2 broth cubes (one beef, one veg for best flavor)
- Salt and pepper, to taste
- 1 tbsp plain flour
- 1 package pre-made pastry (homemade is good too!)

Method:
1. Start by placing the olive oil into a large pan and gently cook the onion and the stewed steak until the steak is just beginning to change color. Stir through the tomato puree.
2. Now add the can of ale and add the same amount of warm water. Crumble the broth cubes into the pan, with the salt and pepper, stir well and then bring to a boil.
3. Reduce the temperature and simmer for an hour.
4. Meanwhile, take a tablespoon of plain flour and place into a bowl with 3 tablespoons water. Stir well to combine, then gently pour into the pan, stirring well.
5. Remove the pan from the heat and set aside.
6. Now open up the packet of pastry and roll it out to fit your pie dish. Cut into two so you have enough for the base and the lid. I like to use ramekins as they are the perfect size, but you can use a regular pie pan, provided it fits into your air fryer.
7. Sprinkle a small amount of flour onto to the ramekin to prevent them from sticking, then press the pastry into the pan(s), followed by the meat mixture, and topped by the pastry lid.
8. Cut a small hole or two in the top of the pie to allow the steam to escape, then cook for 15 minutes at 390°F/200°C.
9. Serve and enjoy!

Inside Out Cheeseburgers

Burgers don't need to be boring and average- they can also be amazing. Especially if you stuff them with cheese and pickles. Yes, really. Try them!

Serves: 2

Ingredients:
- ¾ lb (350g) lean ground beef
- 3 tbsp onion, mixed
- 4 tsp ketchup
- 2 tsp yellow mustard
- Salt and pepper, to taste
- 8 hamburger dill pickle slices
- 4 slices cheddar cheese

Method:
1. Get a large bowl and add the beef, onion, ketchup, mustard, salt and pepper then give it a nice stir to combine.
2. Divide the meat into four, then flatten each into a thin patty.
3. Next place 4 pickle chips and half of the cheese on top of two of the patties. Don't put it right to the edge- you need this extra space to seal.
4. Place the two spare patties on top of the first, then press the edges together firmly.
5. Pop this into the wire basket of your air fryer and cook on 370°F/190°C for 20 minutes. Check halfway through and flip to ensure they cook evenly.

Pork Satay with Peanut Sauce

Peanutty, spicy and melt in the mouth, this pork satay makes a perfect midweek meal which keeps your tummy satisfied, gives your taste buds what they need and gives you that special indulgence you deserve without needing to worry about unhealthy fats or calories.

Serves: 4

Ingredients:
- 1 tsp ground ginger
- 2 tsp hot pepper sauce x2
- 2 cloves garlic, crushed
- 2-3 tbsp sweet soy sauce x2
- 14 oz (400g) lean pork chops, in cubes of 3 cm
- 2 tbsp vegetable oil
- 1 tsp ground coriander
- ¾ cup (200 ml) coconut milk
- 3 ½ oz (100 g) unsalted peanuts, ground

Method:
1. Take a large bowl and mix together the ginger, hot sauce, half the garlic, the soy sauce and the oil. Place the meat into the mixture and leave for at least 15 minutes to marinate.
2. Remove the meat from the marinade and place straight into the wire basket of your air fryer. Cook for 12 minutes on 390°F/200°C, not forgetting to check and turn halfway through to ensure it cooks evenly.
3. Meanwhile, for the peanut sauce, place some oil into a skillet and gently heat up for a few minutes. Then add the garlic and coriander and cook for another minute.
4. Add the coconut milk, peanuts, hot pepper sauce and soy sauce to the pan and bring to the boil. Boil for 5 minutes, stirring often.
5. Remove the pork from the fryer, pour over some of the yummy sauce, then serve and enjoy!

Garlic Butter Pork Chops

Sometimes simple is best. That's why I love these rich, buttery pork chops, lightly flavored with mouth-watering garlic and sprinkled with fresh parsley. These taste brilliant served with a fresh salad and fries, but honestly, they're amazing whatever you put them with!

Serves: 2

Ingredients:
- 1 tbsp butter
- 1 tbsp olive oil
- 2 garlic cloves, finely chopped
- Salt and pepper, to taste
- 2 tsp fresh parsley, chopped
- 4 pork chops

Method:
1. Firstly, melt the butter and olive oil together and then stir through the garlic plus any seasoning you're using.
2. Next, place the pork chops into the bowl and rub the marinade into the pork. Leave to marinate for around an hour.
3. Remove from the fridge and then place them into the wire basket of your air fryer. Cook for 15 minutes on 340°F /175°C, making sure you check them halfway through and turn to ensure they get nicely cooked on both sides.
4. Serve and enjoy!

Sweet and Sour Pork

It's sticky, it's fragrant and it's AMAZING, even if I do say so myself. Using succulent pork cubes teamed with a beautiful homemade sweet and sour sauce, you'll wonder why you ever bothered to get takeaway! Did I mention that it's low-fat and delicious too??

Serves: 4

Ingredients:

For the pork:
- 1 lb (450g) pork cut into cubes
- 1 tsp salt
- ¼ tsp white sugar
- 1 tsp soy sauce
- 1 egg white
- 2 green onions, chopped
- 1/2 cup (55g) corn starch

For the vegetables:
- ½ medium red pepper, cubed
- ½ medium yellow pepper, cubed
- 1 medium onion, cut into wedges
- 1 x 8 oz (225g) can pineapple chunks in syrup (keep the syrup for the sauce)

For the sauce:
- 1 cup (235ml) water
- ¼ tsp salt
- 4 tbsp white sugar
- 4 tbsp ketchup
- 5 tbsp apple cider vinegar
- ½ tsp soy sauce
- 2 tbsp corn starch

Method:

1. Start by cutting the pork into cubes approx. 1" (2cm) in size, then place into a bowl along with the salt, sugar and soy sauce. Stir well to combine. Then add the egg white and green onions and give it all another nice stir to combine. Leave to marinade for approx. an hour. You can skip this bit if you're short on time.
2. Next place the cornstarch into a bowl then remove the pork from the fridge and add to the bowl. Stir through well to coat.

3. Pop the pork into your air fryer to cook for 15 minutes on 350°F/180°C, remembering to check halfway through and turn.
4. Meanwhile, pop some vegetable oil into a skillet and cook the peppers and onions for about 5 minutes until they start to soften. Next add the pineapple chunks (but not the syrup yet), add a sprinkle of salt and sugar and cook until it's all nice and tender.
5. Finally, let's make that sauce. Pop the sauce ingredients (except for the pineapple juice and cornstarch) into a pan and bring to the boil. Add the pepper and onion mix, pork cubes, syrup and the cornstarch and bring to the boil. Cook until soft, sticky and yummy.
6. Serve and enjoy!

Sticky BBQ Pork Strips

More sticky goodness for you! This one is simple, flavorful and utterly delicious. Make the marinade the night before and then you'll have an extra-fast and nutritious meal ready on the table when you get home.

Serves: 3-6

Ingredients:
- 6 pork loin chops
- Freshly ground pepper
- 1 tsp balsamic vinegar
- 2 tbsp soy sauce
- 2 tbsp honey
- 1 clove garlic, finely chopped
- ¼ tsp ground ginger
- Salt and pepper, to taste

Method:
1. Start by placing the pork into a bowl and seasoning with some ground pepper.
2. Follow with the vinegar, soy sauce and honey and mix well to combine. Then add the garlic and ginger and give it another stir to combine. Stir well and leave it all to marinate for an hour of two. You could skip this step but it's definitely worth it!
3. Now place the chops into the wire basket of your air fryer and cook for 15 minutes at 350°F/180°C remembering to turn halfway through to ensure it cooks properly on both sides.
4. Serve and enjoy!

Lamb with Mint and Honey

There's nothing quite as comforting as a rack of lamb, especially when served with love and care. Add roasted potatoes or mash, fresh seasonal vegetable and you have a meal fit for a king. But instead of having to slave away for an hour in the kitchen, you can have this ready within less than half an hour – perfect!

Serves: 4

Ingredients:
- 1 tbsp honey
- ½ cup (100 ml) extra virgin olive oil
- 2 garlic cloves
- 1 bunch fresh mint
- 2 racks of lamb
- Freshly ground pepper

Method:
1. Let's start by making our special mint sauce by placing the honey, oil, garlic and mint into a food processor and blending until smooth.
2. Make a small cut into the lamb racks so you can curl them around into a circle, then spread the mint sauce over the flesh.
3. Transfer to the air fryer and cook for 20 minutes on 370°F/190°C until perfectly cooked. Make sure you check often to turn and smear with extra mint sauce where needed.
4. Serve and enjoy!

Rosemary and Garlic Lamb Cutlets

It's time for more lamb, but this time spiked with rosemary and garlic to give it a Greek twist. The addition of wholegrain mustard really gives the lamb that extra edge that will have you cooking it time and time again.

Serves: 2

Ingredients:
- 1 tbsp honey
- 2 tbsp wholegrain mustard
- 2 tbsp mint sauce
- 2 lamb racks (3 cutlets per rack)
- 2 garlic cloves, finely sliced
- 2 sprigs fresh rosemary

Method:
1. Start by making the marinade. Grab a large bowl and add honey, mustard and mint sauce then stir well to combine. Set to one side.
2. Next make small cuts into the lamb racks and insert slices of garlic and pieces of rosemary into the cuts, and finally brush the lamb with the marinade. Leave for at least 20 minutes for the flavors to infuse.
3. Transfer to the wire basket of your air fryer and cook for 20 minutes on 350°F/180°C. Make sure you check them often and pour some of the sauce over the lamb as it cooks to keep it nice and tender.
4. Slice, serve and enjoy!

Greek Lamb and Spinach Meatballs with Tzatziki

Forget those regular Italian meatballs you've come to know and love, and try these satisfying, mouth-watering lamb, spinach and feta cheese meatballs instead. Infused with more flavor than you can shake a stick at, they're ready fast so you can tuck straight in.

Serves: 4-6 (makes 30 meatballs)

Ingredients:
For the meatballs:
- 2 tbsp olive oil
- 1 cup (150g) minced onion
- 2 cloves minced garlic
- 2 cups (60g) packed chopped spinach
- 1.5 lb (675g) ground lamb
- ½ cup (75g) finely crumbled feta
- 1/3 cup (45g) chopped pine nuts
- 1 tbsp very finely minced fresh oregano
- ½ tsp salt
- 1 egg

For the tzatziki:
- 1 cup (250g) full-fat plain Greek yogurt
- 1/3 cup (50g) diced cucumber
- 2 tbsp chopped fresh dill
- 2 tbsp chopped fresh mint
- 2 tsp lemon juice
- 1 tsp olive oil
- 1-2 cloves garlic

Method:
1. Firstly, take a skillet, add the olive oil and cook the onions for around 5 minutes until softened. Then add the garlic, stir through and cook for a few more minutes. Then add the spinach for just a minute or two and remove from the heat.
2. Place this into a large bowl and add the lamb, feta, pine nuts, oregano, salt, and egg then mix well until all the ingredients are wonderfully combined.
3. Now form your meatballs, either using a large ice cream scoop or simply taking a large spoon of the meat mixture into your hands and form balls.

4. Place into the wire basket of the air fryer and cook at 325°F/ 160°C for 10 minutes until cooked through.
5. Meanwhile, let's make the tzatziki but placing all the ingredients into a bowl and stirring well.
6. Serve with the meatballs and enjoy!

Super-Fast Lamb Roast

Lamb roasts take so much time, don't they? You need to spend all morning locked away in your kitchen to produce one and then you demolish it super-fast, right? Not so with this lamb roast. It's fast, it's easy, and even your 6-year old could make it.

Serves: 4

Ingredients:
- 2 bunches Dutch carrots
- 3 large potatoes, cut into chunks
- 2 tbsp olive oil
- 4 tsp dried rosemary
- 4 tsp garlic, minced
- 4 tsp onion flakes
- 1 lb (450g) lamb roast
- 1 medium sweet potato, peeled and cut into chunks
- 2 cups frozen peas, defrosted in boiling water
- 2 tbsp Instant gravy

Method:
1. Start by trimming your carrots and placing them into a baking tray with the potatoes and a small amount of oil. Place in the oven and cook on 390°F/200°C for 30 minutes.
2. Meanwhile, prepare your lamb. Firstly, place the rosemary, garlic, oil and onion flakes into a small bowl and stir well to combine. Then rub the lamb with this spiced mixture.
3. Place the lamb into a hot skillet and sear the sides until just browned. Season then transfer to your air fryer along with the sweet potato chunks. Cook for 20 minutes on 390°F/200°C.
4. Now remove the carrot and potato mixture from the oven and cover to keep warm. Drain the peas and make the gravy.
5. When the lamb is cooked, remove from the air fryer and allow it to rest for 5-10 minutes. Check the sweet potato, and if it's not quite soft, return to the air fryer.
6. Serve it all together and enjoy!

Poultry

Turkey Breast with Maple Mustard Glaze

Roasted turkey isn't just for Thanksgiving- it can be for any time of year, especially when it's this easy! Gently flavored with herbs and coated with a deliciously sweet glaze, you'll wish you'd discovered this recipe before. Promise.

Serves: 6

Ingredients:
- 1 tsp dried thyme
- ½ tsp dried sage
- ½ tsp smoked paprika
- 1 tsp salt
- ½ tsp freshly ground black pepper
- 5 lb (2.2kg) whole turkey breast
- 2 tsp olive oil
- 4 tbsp maple syrup
- 2 tbsp Dijon mustard
- 1 tbsp butter

Method:
1. Start by preparing the spice mix by taking a small bowl and mixing together the thyme, sage, paprika, and salt and pepper. Give it a good stir to combine well.
2. Now brush your turkey with the olive oil then follow this by rubbing the spice mix on top.
3. Transfer the turkey to the air fryer and cook for 25-30 minutes on 350°F/170°C. Make sure you check midway though and turn to ensure it cooks all over.
4. Meanwhile, take a small saucepan and add the maple syrup, mustard and butter. Turn on the heat and melt over a low heat, stirring constantly. Set to one side.
5. Remove your cooked turkey from the oven and brush with the glaze that you just made.
6. Pop back into the air fryer for 5 more minutes, remove and rest for another 5 then serve and enjoy!

Turkey & Cheese Calzone

Whenever I make calzones, I usually stick to the usual pepperoni-cheese-tomato combo, but these little beauties certainly changed the game. You can use leftover turkey from Thanksgiving (yay- no more turkey sandwiches!), and create an awesome meal with the minimum of effort. Note: This recipe uses frozen pizza dough, but you can use your own if you'd prefer.

Serves: 4

Ingredients:
- 1 package frozen pizza dough
- 1 tsp dried oregano
- 1 tsp basil
- 1 tsp thyme
- Salt & pepper, to taste
- 4 tbsp tomato sauce
- Cooked turkey, shredded
- 1 oz (25g) bacon, diced
- 1 cup (100g) cheddar cheese, grated
- ¼ cup (25g) mozzarella cheese, grated
- 1 free-range egg, beaten

Method:
1. Firstly, open up that pizza dough and roll into small circles, the same size as a small pizza.
2. Next, place the oregano, basil and thyme into a bowl with tomato sauce and mix well to combine.
3. Pour a small amount of this sauce onto your pizza bases and spread across the surface using the back of a spoon. Keep away from the edges through- you'll need this bit to help them stick.
4. And then we get to the best part- layering up! Place inside the turkey, bacon and cheese, keeping to just one side of the circle. Brush the edge with the beaten egg, then fold over and pinch to seal. Brush the outside with more egg, then place into the air fryer.
5. Cook on 350°F/180°C for 10 minutes, checking halfway through and turning often.

Turkey Meatballs

You haven't eaten meatballs until you've tried this ingenious recipe. Using crushed chips for extra crunch and flavor, a handful of spices and more leftover turkey from Thanksgiving, they taste amazing. Not that you'll be able to wait until Thanksgiving to make these- they're awesome.

Serves: 2-4

Ingredients:
- 1 cup (35g) crushed chips
- 1 tbsp Montreal steak spice
- 1 tbsp onion flakes
- 1 tbsp dried garlic
- Salt and pepper, to taste
- 2 packages ground turkey
- 2 cloves garlic, crushed
- 2-3 free-range eggs

Method:
1. Take a medium bowl and throw in the chips, the spices and the salt and pepper. Mix well to combine.
2. Now grab another bowl and add the meat, the garlic, eggs, and mix well to combine. Once you're happy that it's nicely mixed, add the chip mixture from the medium bowl and mix again.
3. Using your hands, shape into meatballs of a size you'd love then throw into your air fryer.
4. Spray a small amount of oil inside and then cook for 10 minutes on 350°F/180°C, turning often to ensure they cook all over.
5. Serve and enjoy!

Ultimate Southern Fried Chicken

Fast, delicious and almost totally mess free, this crunchy southern fried chicken packs in the taste, satisfies you hunger like nothing else in the world, and lights up your soul!

Serves: 4

Ingredients:
- 8-10 chicken drumettes
- 1 cup (235ml) buttermilk
- 2 cups (240g) white flour
- 1 tbsp salt
- 1 tbsp black pepper
- 1 tbsp garlic powder
- 1 tsp creole seasoning
- 1 tsp onion powder
- 1 tbsp paprika
- 1 tsp cumin

Method:
1. Firstly, we need to marinate the chicken in the buttermilk for an hour or two in the fridge.
2. Meanwhile, place the flour into a large bowl, add the seasoning and stir well to combine.
3. After the marinating time has passed, remove from the fridge, remove the chicken from the buttermilk and place onto a plate.
4. Take each in turn and dip into the flour mixture, rubbing in to coat completely. Then dip into the buttermilk. Then again into the flour.
5. Place into the air fryer basket then cook at 360°F/180°C for 20 minutes, turning often to make sure it all cooks through.
6. Serve and enjoy!

Tandoori Chicken Legs

Get your hungry crew rounded up for these awesome Indian-inspired chicken dish. Perfect for a main meal when served with a big salad and rice, or delicious as a snack when you're there watching Netflix, they'll definitely become your go-to chicken dish.

Serves: 2-4

Ingredients:
- 4 chicken legs
- Salt, to taste
- ½ tsp ginger-garlic paste
- ½ tsp chili paste
- ¼ tsp garam masala
- ¼ cumin powder
- ¼ tsp ground coriander
- Juice of a lime
- 2 tbsp yogurt
- 1 tsp oil

Method:
1. Start by making small slices into your chicken legs and placing to one side.
2. Then take a bowl and add the salt, ginger-garlic paste, chili, garam masala, cumin, coriander, lime juice and yogurt. It will look messy but wait for the magic to happen! Give it a mix and watch it transform.
3. Now smear the chicken legs with the yogurt and leave to rest for a few hours so the flavors can really infuse.
4. Pop into the air fryer and cook for 15 minutes on 390°F/200°C. Don't forget to check and turn halfway through.
5. Serve and enjoy!

Momma's Best Chicken Nuggets

For me, the very best thing about these chicken nuggets is that almond flour-parmesan crust which lifts this recipe right up from average to awesome. The name comes from the face that the recipe was originally my mothers, but I've given it a facelift for the air fryer. Enjoy!

Serves: 4-6

Ingredients:
- 1 ¼ lb (560g) boneless skinless chicken breasts
- 1 large free-range egg, well beaten
- ½ cup (50g) almond flour
- ¼ cup (25g) parmesan cheese
- 1 tsp sea salt
- ½ tsp black pepper
- 1 tsp regular or smoked paprika

Method:
1. Start by cutting your chicken breasts into three pieces across the breast. Place to one side.
2. Now take a bowl, add the egg and beat well. Add the chicken to the bowl and toss to coat completely.
3. Grab another large bowl and add the almond flour, cheese, salt, pepper and paprika and mix them well to combine. Pop the chicken into the flour mixture and toss well to coat. Yum!
4. Place into your air fryer and back for 390/200 for 15-20 minutes, turning often.
5. Serve and enjoy!

Spiced Turkey Curry Samosas

These have to be the easiest samosas I've ever made or tasted. But don't be deceived- they might be so simple that you could get your 3-year old to make but they're very very VERY tasty. Feel free to play with this recipe- why not add grated carrots, peas, and even small pieces of potato to add some depth and variety to the mix?

Serves: 8

Ingredients:
- 1 tsp garam masala
- 1 tsp turmeric
- 1 tsp coriander
- Salt & pepper, to taste
- Drop of coconut milk (regular milk will do)
- 2 sheets pastry
- 1 ½ oz (50g) turkey wing meat, shredded
- 1 free-range egg, beaten

Method:
1. Take a large mixing bowl and throw in all the ingredients (apart from the pastry and the egg), then stir well to combine. You can add a drop of coconut milk to keep everything moist, but this isn't mandatory.
2. Now open up those pastry sheets and cut into small pieces.
3. Place some of the filling mixture into the pastry pieces and fold over to close. Feel free to experiment with this bit and make them whatever size and shape you want.
4. Brush with the beaten egg and place straight into the air fryer.
5. Cook for 5 minutes at 320°F/160°C.
6. Serve and enjoy!!

Gluten-Free Mexican Chicken Burgers

Most burgers, 'fried' meat dishes and those in breadcrumbs are coated in crispy high-carb goodness. But not these chicken burgers. Using ground cauliflower instead of breadcrumbs, these burgers are gluten-free, Paleo and Keto friendly and pretty darn good too!

Serves: 4

Ingredients:
- 3 tbsp smoked paprika
- 1 tbsp dried thyme
- 1 tbsp oregano
- 1 tbsp mustard powder
- 1 tsp cayenne pepper
- 1 jalapeno pepper
- 1 small cauliflower
- 1 free-range egg, beaten
- 4 chicken breasts, skin and bones removed
- Salt & Pepper

Method:
1. Start by putting the seasoning into a blender with the cauliflower and hit that blend button until it looks like breadcrumbs. Divide the mixture into two bowls - one with ¾ of the crumbs, and the other ¼ into a bowl.
2. Beat the egg in another bowl and set aside.
3. Using your blender again and add the chicken plus the ¼ mixture of cauliflower and seasonings. Add some salt and pepper if needed.
4. Form into burger shapes using your hands, then dip into the egg, then roll in the cauli-crumbs. Repeat for all of them.
5. Cook for 30 minutes for 350°F/180°C, turning halfway through to ensure they cook evenly.

Fast and Easy Chicken Kiev

Ooozing with delicious garlicky soft cheese, the chicken Kiev is simply unforgettable. They're also fast, easy and taste perfect with almost anything.

Serves: 2

Ingredients:
- ½ cup (115g) garlic and herb flavor soft cheese
- 1 tsp fresh parsley
- ¼ tsp garlic puree
- 2 chicken breasts
- Breadcrumbs
- Salt & pepper, to taste
- 1 free-range egg, beaten

Method:
1. Firstly, take a medium bowl and add the soft cheese, half the parsley and the garlic and stir well to combine, then set to one side.
2. Next take a rolling pin and flatten each of the chicken breasts, then carefully cut in half.
3. Take half the mixture and place into the middle of the chicken, then top with the other half of the chicken breast. Repeat with the other chicken breast.
4. Grab another bowl and add the breadcrumbs, salt, pepper and the rest of the parsley then stir well to combine. Place the beaten egg in another bowl.
5. Cover the chicken in beaten egg, then roll in the breadcrumbs, and pop into your air fryer.
6. Cook on 350°F/180°C for 25-30 minutes, turning often to ensure they cook properly.
7. Serve and enjoy!

Whole Roasted Chicken

Next time, skip the oven and make roasted chicken right there in your air fryer. It tastes even better, it's clean and it's very easy indeed.

Serves: 4

Ingredients:
- 3 lb. (1.5kg) whole chicken
- 1 tbsp olive oil
- Salt & pepper, to taste
- 1 tbsp mixed herbs
- 1 onion, chopped in half

Method:
1. Start by drying off the chicken, then gently coat with the olive oil, salt, pepper and herbs.
2. Next remove the giblets from the chicken (if not already done) and in its place put both the halved onions.
3. Now place into the basket of your air fryer upside down and cook for 40 minutes on 330°F/170°C, turning often to cook thoroughly.

Simply The Best Chicken Schnitzel

Schnitzel is simply chicken seasoned with a touch of mustard and salt and pepper, before being fried until crispy and tasty. Enjoy this healthy, gluten-free version and tell your friends all about it!

Serves: 4

Ingredients:
- 2 chicken breasts
- Salt & pepper, to taste
- 2 free-range eggs
- 12 tbsp gluten-free oats
- 2 tbsp mustard powder
- Fresh parsley

Method:
1. Start by carefully slicing your chicken into two lengthwise and then rolling out with a rolling pin until flat.
2. Sprinkle with salt and pepper and place to one side.
3. Next break two eggs into a small bowl and whisk well, set to one side.
4. Grind those oats in your blender along with the mustard, parsley and salt and pepper. You want it to become like breadcrumbs. Place into another shallow dish.
5. Take each piece of chicken and dip into the egg until well coated, then into the oaty breadcrumb mixture.
6. Pop into your air fryer and cook for 12 minutes at 350°F/ 180°C. Don't forget to turn hallway though to make sure it cooks well on both sides.
7. Serve with German-style potatoes for best results. And enjoy!

Healthy Cheesy-Fried Chicken

Enjoy this very special chicken, oozing with mozzarella cheese and flavored with extra Parmesan and marinara sauce. It's healthier than you think and tastes out of this world.

Serves: 4

Ingredients:
- 2 x 8oz (225g) chicken breast
- 6 tbsp seasoned breadcrumbs
- 2 tbsp grated Parmesan cheese
- 1 tbsp olive oil
- 1/2 cup (115g) Marinara sauce
- 6 tbsp reduced fat mozzarella cheese

Method:
1. Start by carefully slicing the chicken breast into two, horizontally to make four pieces then set to one side.
2. Place the breadcrumbs into a bowl with the Parmesan and stir well to combine, set to one side.
3. Now brush your chicken pieces with the olive oil, then dip into the breadcrumbs.
4. Place into your air fryer and cook for 10 minutes on 360°F/ 180°C.
5. Remove from the air fryer and top with 1 tablespoon of the marinara sauce and 1 tablespoon of the mozzarella cheese. Cook for 3 more minutes until the cheese has melted.
6. Serve and enjoy!

Chick-fil-A Chicken Sandwich

You might recognize this copycat recipe, inspired by the Atlanta-based Chick-Fil-A brand so you'll be pleased to hear you can recreate exactly the same amazing taste right there in your kitchen with your air fryer. Yay! It's much lower in fat too.

Serves: 2

Ingredients:
- 2 chicken breasts, Boneless/Skinless
- ½ cup (115ml) dill pickle juice
- 2 free-range eggs
- ½ cup (115ml) milk
- 1 cup (120g) flour
- 2 tbsp powdered sugar
- 1 tsp paprika
- 1 tsp salt
- ½ tsp black pepper
- ½ tsp garlic powder
- ¼ tsp ground celery seed
- 1 tbsp olive oil

To serve:
- 4 hamburger buns toasted and buttered
- 8 Dill pickle
- Mayonnaise

Method:
1. Start by placing the chicken onto your work surface and pound until it's about ½ inch/1.5cm thick. Now cut your chicken into 2 to 3 pieces- it's up to you!
2. Place the chicken into a large bowl, pour over the pickle juice and leave to marinate for around 30 minutes.
3. Meanwhile, take another bowl, break in the egg, followed by the milk and beat well until combined.
4. Then take another bowl and combine the flour and spices.
5. Finally, remove your chicken from the marinade and pop into the egg mixture followed by the flour.
6. Transfer to your air fryer and cook at 340°F/ 170°C degrees for 12 minutes. Don't forget to check and turn half way through.
7. Meanwhile, toast and butter your buns and then serve with the chicken, pickles and mayonnaise. ENJOY!

Chicken and Mushroom Pie

Now it's time for something completely different- PIE! This one is brilliant if you've never made pie before and you want to impress, or if you're a seasoned pro and want to save time in the kitchen whilst still serving up amazing food.

Serves: 4

Ingredients

- 2 chicken thighs, cubed
- Soy sauce
- Pepper, to taste
- 1 tsp olive oil
- 1 onion, diced
- 1 carrot, diced
- 2 small potatoes, diced
- Salt, to taste
- 1 tsp Italian mixed dried herbs
- ½ teaspoon garlic powder
- Worcestershire sauce, to taste
- 1 tbsp plain flour
- Milk, as required
- 2 sheets puff pastry
- 2 hard-boiled eggs
- Melted butter

Method:

1. Start by placing the chicken cubes into a large bowl and adding the soy sauce and pepper. Leave to marinate whilst you prepare the rest.
2. Meanwhile, take a skillet, add a small amount of olive oil and fry the onion, carrot and potatoes. When it starts to stick, add some water, followed by the chicken cubes.
3. Top with the salt, pepper, dried herbs, garlic powder and Worcestershire sauce and stir. Add with more liquid as required.
4. Sprinkle with plain flour and stir through. Add a drop of milk and continue to simmer until the vegetables are perfectly cooked.

5. Now find a non-stick baking tray that will fit your air fryer (or use the one provided) and place one sheet of puff pastry inside. Press down into the bottom, and use a fork to press some holes into the base to allow steam to escape.
6. Next, pour in the cooked filling and top with your peeled, chopped hard-boiled eggs.
7. Lay the second piece of pastry over the top, brush with the melted butter and poke some holes at the center to allow steam to escape.
8. Pop into your air fryer and cook for 6-10 minutes on 350°F/180°C. Check throughout to make sure you catch the pie when it's perfectly cooked.
9. Serve and enjoy!

Spiced Buttermilk Chicken

This spiced buttermilk chicken is a cut above the rest. Yes, you will need to be organized and start preparing beforehand, but it's very much worth it! You can also turn up the heat by adding chili powder or extra black pepper. Yum!

Serves: 4-6

Ingredients:
For the chicken:
- 1.7 lb (800g) chicken thighs, skin on
- 2 tsp black pepper
- 2 tsp salt
- 1 tsp paprika powder 2 cups buttermilk

For the seasoned flour:
- 2 cups flour
- 1 tbsp baking powder
- 1 tbsp garlic powder
- 1 tbsp paprika
- 1 tsp salt

Method:
1. Start by drying the chicken and then placing into a large bowl. Add the pepper, paprika and salt then pour over the buttermilk. Put into the fridge for a few hours or overnight.
2. Take a separate bowl, add the ingredients for the seasoned flour: the flour, baking powder, garlic powder, paprika and salt. Mix well to combine.
3. Now remove the chicken from the buttermilk and put into the seasoned flour. Shake off any excess and place into the wire basket of your air fryer. Repeat with the remaining pieces.
4. Cook for 15-20 minutes on 350°F/180°C until perfectly cooked.
5. Serve and enjoy!

Southern Hot Chicken

Talking of heat...let's get things steamin' with this southern-fried hot chicken. It will get your eyes watering and your tongue on fire, but if you're a fan of spicy food, you will LOVE it. Promise!

Serves: 4

Ingredients:
For the chicken:
- 4 chicken breasts
- 2 free-range eggs
- 1 cup (235ml) buttermilk
- 2 cups (240g) flour
- 2 tbsp paprika
- 1 tsp garlic powder
- 1 tsp onion powder
- 2 tsp salt
- 1 tsp freshly ground black pepper

For the hot sauce:
- 1 tbsp cayenne pepper
- 1 tsp salt
- 4 tbsp vegetable oil

To serve:
- 4 slices white bread
- Dill pickle slices

Method:
1. Start by cutting the chicken breasts into 2 pieces so you have a total of 8 pieces now, pop to one side.
2. Take a medium bowl and add the eggs and buttermilk then whisk together.
3. In another bowl, combine the flour, paprika, garlic powder, onion powder, salt and pepper and stir well.
4. Finally, dip your chicken into the egg mixture followed by the flour. Repeat with the remaining chicken. Ensure all sides of the chicken are completely covered.
5. Pop into your air fryer and cook on 370°F/190°C for 20-25 minutes. Don't forget to flip them half way through. Remove from the air fryer.

6. Meanwhile, take a small bowl and combine the cayenne pepper and salt, stirring well to combine. Warm the oil and add this to the spice mixture, stirring well.
7. Now build your sandwich by placing the chicken on the bread, pour over the hot sauce and top with the pickle slices.
8. Serve and enjoy!

Chinese Chicken Wings

For those days when you walk through the door and just want to eat something easy, open up your fridge and create these Chinese chicken wings. They're salty, spicy and sooo satisfying.

Serves: 2

Ingredients:
- 1 tbsp soy sauce
- 1 tsp mixed spice
- 1 tbsp Chinese spice
- Salt & pepper, to taste
- 4 chicken wings

Method:
1. Start by placing the soy sauce, mixed spice, Chinese spice and seasoning into a large bowl and stir well to combine.
2. Add the chicken wings and make sure they're beautifully covered.
3. Place a piece of silver foil into the bottom of your air fryer, place the chicken on top and then pour the rest of the seasoning on top.
4. Cook for 30 minutes on 350°F/180°C.
5. Serve and enjoy!

Prawn Paste Chicken

If you've never tried prawn paste chicken, then prepare to think you've died and gone to heaven! This one combines real Chinese flavor including prawns, sesame and ginger to make a real treat for your taste buds.

Serves: 2-3

Ingredients:
- 2 tbsp olive oil
- 1 tbsp prawn/shrimp paste
- ¾ tsp sugar
- 1 tsp sesame oil
- ½ tsp dried ginger
- 2/3 lb (300g) chicken wings

Method:
1. Take a large bowl and combine all the ingredients, except for the chicken. Stir well to combine then place the chicken on top. Leave for as long as you can- at least an hour but preferably overnight.
2. Remove from the marinade and place in your air fryer. Cook on 350°F/180°C for 5 minutes. Lightly brush with olive oil then place back into the air fryer for a further 15 minutes. Turn midway through to ensure the chicken is cooking on both sides.
3. Serve and enjoy!

Indian Chili Chicken

This Indian Chili chicken is served with the best spicy sauce I've ever tried. Seriously. Combining a well-balance spectrum of flavors, you'll lick your lips and feel beautifully satisfied when you've finished. Simply serve with plain rice and boom- the perfect meal is yours!

Serves: 4

Ingredients:
- 2/3 lb (300g) boneless and skinless chicken thighs, cut into small bite size pieces
- 2 tbsp corn flour
- 1 tbsp plain flour
- ½ tsp chili powder
- ½ tsp ground pepper
- 1 tsp garlic and ginger paste
- Pinch of salt
- 1 tbsp vinegar
- 3 tbsp water

For the sauce:
- 2 tbsp vegetable oil
- 4 spring onions finely chopped
- 1 green chili, cut in three
- 8-10 cloves garlic, finely chopped
- ½" (1.5cm) ginger, finely chopped
- 7 oz (220g) green pepper, diced
- 3 oz (80g) red onion diced
- 1 tbsp chili garlic sauce
- 1 tbsp soy sauce
- 3 tbsp water
- 1 tsp corn flour mixed with 2 tsp of water
- Salt, to taste

Method:
1. Let's start by making the batter for your chicken. Take a large bowl and add the corn flour, plain flour, chili, pepper, salt and ginger-garlic paste. Give it all a mix to combine.
2. Then add the vinegar and water and stir well to create a batter.

3. Now drop the chicken into the batter and move around until the chicken is well coated.
4. Pop into the air fryer and cook for 15 minutes on 350°F/180°C. Check halfway to ensure it's evenly cooked.
5. Meanwhile, let's make the sauce. Take a skillet and fry the onions, chili, garlic and ginger together for a few seconds. Then add the peppers and red onions and cook for 2-3 minutes.
6. Now add the soy sauce and chili garlic sauce and stir well, followed by the water and simmer for 1 minute on a low heat. Turn down, add the cornflower batter (the one you used before) and simmer for 2 minutes. Then turn the heat off and allow to cool. This is your sauce.
7. Now add the chicken to the sauce and simmer for a minute, then serve and enjoy!

Awesome Piri-Piri Chicken

This recipe is super-quick and also super-tasty. Serve with a vat of red wine and a lot of love. It's perfectly spicy and wonderful for small intimate meals and big gatherings.

Serves: 3-4

Ingredients:
- 1 whole chicken
- 1 ½ cup (400 ml) olive oil
- 5/8 cup (150ml) tomato sauce
- 1 tbsp garlic puree
- 1 tbsp paprika
- 1 tbsp fresh parsley
- 1 tbsp piri piri seasoning
- Salt & pepper, to taste

Method:
1. Firstly, cut your chicken in half and place onto a large sheet of silver foil.
2. Now place everything on your ingredients list (apart from that chicken) into a blender and blend until it's finely chopped and combined.
3. Brush this over the chicken on both sides, cover with extra salt and pepper and then pop into the fridge for an hour.
4. After the hour has passed, place into your air fryer (the foil too) and cook for 25 minutes on 350°F/ 180°C. Make sure you turn it halfway through to ensure it all cooks on both sides.
5. Serve and enjoy!

Seafood

Battered White Fish with Tangy Lemon Sauce

If you're in the mood for something a little different, try this tangy and sweet fish dish. The fish itself is beautifully crispy and the lemon sauce adds something extra special to this dish. Try it!

Serves: 4

Ingredients:
- 1 fresh lemon
- 4 tbsp sugar
- 1 ¼ cup flour
- 2 tsp green chili sauce
- 2 tsp oil
- 1 egg white
- 2 pieces white fish, cut into 4 pieces
- 1 tbsp syrup
- Salt, to taste
- 4 tsp corn flour, mixed with a small amount of water
- 1 tsp red chili sauce
- Juice of one lemon
- 2-3 lettuce leave, to serve

Method:
1. Start by slicing your lemon and placing into the bottom of a bowl. Set aside.
2. Place ½ cup water into a pan, add the sugar and stir until it dissolves. Place to one side.
3. Now place 1 cup of the flour, the green chili sauce, oil and egg white into a bowl and mix well. Add 2-3 tablespoons water and whisk well to make a batter.
4. Now sprinkle some flour onto a separate plate and set to one side. Now we're ready to work on the fish!
5. Start by dipping the fish into your batter then allow any excess to drip away. Next place them on the plate with the flour and coat well with the flour.
6. Cook in your air fryer for 20-25 minutes on 350°F/ 180°C and make sure you turn halfway through to cook well on both sides.
7. Meanwhile let's continue with that sauce. Take your pan with the syrup and mix in the salt, the corn flour-water mixture and blend. Then add the red chili sauce, lemon slices, lemon juice and mix well. Cook until it gets lovely and thick.
8. Serve together and enjoy!

Crispy Cod Nuggets with Lemon Honey Tartar Sauce

Tell your kids to skip McDonald's and get them to help you make these nutritious, simple and delicious cod nuggets instead of eating junk-rich processed food. They're ready incredibly quickly, and the tartar sauce really is something special.

Serves: 2-4

Ingredients:
For the fish:
- 1 cup 925g) cornflake crumbs
- 1 tbsp vegetable oil
- ½ cup (60g) flour
- Salt and pepper, to season
- 1 free-range egg + 1 tablespoon water
- 1 lb. (450g) cod fillet, cut in about 6-8 chunks

For the Lemon Honey Tartar Sauce:
- ½ cup (115g) mayonnaise
- 1 tsp honey
- Zest of half a lemon, finely minced
- Juice of half a lemon
- ½ tsp Worcestershire sauce
- 1 tbsp sweet pickle relish
- Pinch black pepper

Method:
1. Firstly, place the corn flakes into a food processor and crush until fine. Next add the vegetable oil and pulse again until combined.
2. Sprinkle the flour onto a plate and add the salt and pepper, and stir well to combine then place to one side. Then break the egg into a separate bowl and whisk well.
3. Now take the fish and place into the flour mixture, rubbing until coated. Remove, dust off the excess then transfer to the egg. Make sure everything is well coated. Finally, place into the cornflake crumbs and cover well.
4. Pop into the air fryer for 15 minutes on 350°F/ 180°C. Turn halfway through cooking.
5. Meanwhile, make the tartar sauce by popping all the ingredients into a blender, hitting the whizz button and popping it into the fridge until the cod is ready.
6. Serve all together and enjoy!

Battered Fish and Chips

Feel like you've caught an airplane and headed across the Atlantic when you tuck into these British-style Fish and chips. However, unlike the British version, these have been pimped with garlic and dill to give that flavor-full US touch.

Serves: 4

Ingredients:

- 2 lb. (1kg) Maris Piper potatoes
- ½ cup (100g) flour
- 1 tsp baking soda
- 1 tsp lemon pepper
- Good pinch dried dill
- 1/2 tsp garlic granules
- Salt and pepper, to taste
- 4 cod loin fillets
- ½ cup (120ml) water
- 2 tsp olive oil

Method:

1. For chips, peel off the skins and cut the potatoes into chip shapes then rinse, dry and pop into your air fryer for 45 minutes at 350°F/ 180°C. For best results, add a touch of oil.
2. For the fish, take a bowl and combine the flour with the baking soda, herbs, garlic, salt and pepper and stir well to combine.
3. Place the fish into the seasoned flour and coat well. Leave to rest for 10 minutes or so. After 10 minutes or so, take out the fish from seasoned flour and set aside.
4. Next make a batter by gently pouring a small amount of water into the seasoned flour and whisking well until smooth. Try to keep the batter relatively thick for best results.
5. Pop the fish into the batter then place into the air fryer with a touch of olive oil. Cook for 20 minutes. If you have smaller air fryer, you might need to cook the chips and the fish separately. Simply keep those chips warm by popping into a warm over and/or covering.
6. Serve and enjoy!

Blackened Shrimp

When these babies hit your tongue, you'll experience the most intense flavor ever. Perfectly balanced with warm spices, herbs and chili, these shrimp will vanish from the plate.

Serves: 2-4

Ingredients:
- 20 jumbo shrimps
- 2 tbsp oil
- 2 tsp cilantro
- 2 tsp smoked paprika
- 2 tsp onion powder
- 2 tsp garlic powder
- 1 tsp cumin
- 1 tsp sea salt
- 1 tsp black pepper
- 1 tsp thyme
- 1 tsp oregano
- ¼ tsp cayenne pepper
- ¼ tsp red chili flakes

Method:
1. Grab a large bowl and add the seasonings, then stir well to combine.
2. Place the shrimp onto a flat surface and brush gently with the oil, then pop into the spice mix. Stir well to coat then transfer to the wire basket of your air fryer.
3. Cook for 10 minutes on 350°F/ 180°C until crisp. Don't forget to check and turn halfway through.
4. Serve and enjoy!

Thai Fish Cakes with Mango Salsa

I love the way Thai cuisine mixes sweet and savory. In this dish, we have light coconut, chili, citrus, cilantro, onion and of course light and fluffy fish, coated in a crunchy coconut crust. What could be better?

Serves: 4

Ingredients:
- 1 ripe mango
- 1 ½ tsp red chili paste
- 3 tbsp fresh cilantro
- Juice and zest of 1 lime
- 1 lb. (450g) white fish fillet
- 1 free-range egg
- 1 tsp salt
- 1 green onion, finely chopped
- 2 oz (55g) ground coconut

Method
1. Peel the mango, cut around the stone and dice into small cubes. Place into a bowl with ½ teaspoon of the red chili paste, 1 tablespoon of the cilantro and the juice and zest of half a lime. Stir well to combine then set to one side.
2. Now let's do the fish. Place the fish into a food processor and hit blend until smooth. Open up the lid and add the egg, the salt and the rest of the lime zest, chili paste, lime juice, cilantro, onion and 2 tablespoons of the coconut. Whizz until combined.
3. Take the fish and divide into approximately 12 balls, then roll in the remaining coconut.
4. Place into your air fryer and cook for 7-10 minutes 350°F/ 180°C until browned. Remember to check them halfway through and turn if necessary.
5. Serve with the spicy mango salsa and ENJOY!

Cajun Shrimp

Tiger shrimp are big, tasty and work incredibly well when coated with Cajun spiced and gently cooked for five minutes in your air fryer. Perfect for a snack, a supper or a romantic nibble.

Serves: 4-6

Ingredients:
- 16-20 tiger shrimp
- ¼ tsp cayenne pepper
- ½ tsp old bay seasoning
- ¼ teaspoon smoked paprika
- 1 pinch of salt
- 1 tbsp olive oil

Method:
1. Take a large bowl and add the seasonings then give them a good stir to combine.
2. Then place the shrimp into the spice mixture, stir to coat and pop into your air fryer.
3. Cook for just 5 minutes on 350°F/ 180°C then serve and enjoy! See? I told you these were fast!

Herb and Garlic Fish Fingers

Wave your magic wand over a US classic by creating these beautifully spiced fish fingers. Don't let the list of spices put you off- they're actually much than they look and taste brilliant. Reduce the chili is you're making these for kids (or not if they like some spice!) and enjoy the surprised looks on their faces.

Serves: 4

Ingredients:
- ½ tsp salt
- 2 tbsp lemon juice
- ½ tsp turmeric powder
- ½ tsp red chili flakes
- ½ tsp pepper
- 1 tsp ginger garlic paste
- 2 tsp mixed dried herbs (1 + 1 tsp)
- 2 tsp garlic powder (1 + 1 tsp)
- 10 oz (300g) fish, cut into fingers
- 2 tbsp flour
- 2 tsp corn flour
- 2 free-range eggs
- ¼ tsp baking soda
- 1 cup (50g) breadcrumbs
- Olive oil, for brushing

Method:
1. Start by grabbing a large bowl and add the salt, lemon juice, turmeric, chili, pepper, the ginger-garlic paste, 1 teaspoon of the herbs and 1 teaspoon of the garlic powder. Stir well to combine.
2. Add the fish to the spice mixture and leave to rest for 10 minutes.
3. Meanwhile, mix the flour, corn flour, egg and baking soda in another bowl.
4. Remove the fish from the spice marinade and transfer to the flour and egg mixture. Ensure it's well covered.
5. Finally, combine the remaining mixed herbs and garlic powder with the breadcrumbs, and add the fish. Stir well to coat.
6. Pop into the air fryer and cook for 350°F/ 180°C for 10-15 minutes, turning often.
7. Serve and enjoy.

Mustard & Spring Onion Crab Cakes

Whenever I bite into one of these crab cakes, I can't help but think of my lovely grandmother who used to serve up these delicious treats every time we used to visit her home as kids. They're light, full of flavor and they taste amazing with tomato ketchup.

Serves: 2-4

Ingredients:
- 2 free-range eggs
- 2 tbsp mayonnaise
- 1 tsp Dijon mustard
- 1 ½ tsp Old Bay seasoning
- 1 tsp Worcestershire sauce
- ¼ cup (40g) spring onion, finely chopped
- ¼ cup (5g) parsley, finely chopped
- Fresh pepper to taste
- 1 lb (450g) crabmeat
- ½ cup (25g) breadcrumbs

Method:
1. Start by grabbing a medium bowl and adding the egg, mayonnaise, mustard, old bay seasoning, Worcestershire sauce, spring onion and parsley. Give it all a nice mix to combine well.
2. Then add the crabmeat to the mix and stir well again. Finally, add the breadcrumbs and stir again.
3. Pop into the fridge for at least an hour to let the flavors infuse and for it to firm up.
4. When they're rested for a while, remove from the fridge and shape into crab cakes. I like to make 8 large ones, but feel free to play with the size and shape.
5. Cook in your air fryer for 10 minutes at 350°F/ 180°C.
6. Serve and enjoy. Ketchup optional.

Shrimp & Oyster Tempura

Treat yourself to something slightly more mature and special with this shrimp and oyster tempura. You can use whatever seafood you like (provided you've chopped it into chunks) and really indulge your sense and your taste buds. Get it right and you should have light, delicately crunchy chunks of the most incredible food on earth.

Serves: 2-4

Ingredients:
- 1/8 tsp baking soda
- ½ tsp kosher salt
- ¼ cup (25g) cornstarch
- ¾ cup (80g) flour
- 1 egg yolk
- 1 cup (235ml) sparkling water (ice cold)
- 1 lb (450g) seafood, cut into chunks

Method:
1. Start by warming your air fryer to 400°F/ 205°C.
2. Before we start, remember that tempura is about speed, heat, light and air. Got it? Great! Let's get started.
3. Grab a large bowl and add the dry ingredients. Give them a stir to ensure they're well-mixed.
4. When your air fryer is hot, whisk the egg and sparkling water together then pour into the bowl of dry ingredients. Mix well to combine.
5. Quickly drop the seafood into the batter, stir well then pop into your air fryer as quickly as you can. Cook for 2-4 minutes.
6. Serve and enjoy! Tastes great with champagne or sparkling wine. Yum!

Coconut Shrimp with Spicy Marmalade Sauce

When I first came across this recipe, I was pretty cynical about whether it would work. Marmalade? With shrimp? Well, it turns out that I needn't have worried. The coconut adds a gentle sweetness and depth to the shrimp and the spicy marmalade sauce is lip-lickingly good.

Serves: 2

Ingredients:
- 8 large shrimps
- 8 oz. (235ml) coconut milk
- ¼ tsp salt
- ¼ tsp ground pepper
- ½ cup (30g) shredded, sweetened coconut
- ½ tsp cayenne pepper
- ½ cup (25g) breadcrumbs
- ½ cup (160g) orange marmalade
- 1 tbsp honey
- 1 tsp mustard
- ¼ tsp hot sauce

Method:
1. Start by shelling, deveining and cleaning the shrimp and pop to one side.
2. Now grab a small bowl and add the coconut milk and salt and pepper. Pop to one side.
3. Taking another bowl. Combine the coconut, cayenne pepper, salt, pepper and breadcrumbs. Stir well to combine, then set to one side.
4. Now dip the shrimp into the coconut milk, then the breadcrumbs, then transfer to the air fryer.
5. Cook for 20 minutes on 350°F/ 180°C, turning halfway through to cook evenly.
6. Meanwhile, pop the marmalade, honey, mustard and hot sauce together in a bowl and serve with the cooked shrimp.
7. Enjoy!

Easy Tuna Cutlets

I love those meals when open your fridge, notice that you have a ton of leftovers and use them to create something tasty, easy and brilliant! Such as these great tuna cutlets. They're ready fast and taste awesome serves with buckets of hot chili sauce!

Serves: 1-2

Ingredients:
- ½ tbsp oil plus extra for brushing
- 1 onion, chopped
- 1 green chili, seeded and chopped
- 1 tsp ground ginger
- 1 small can tuna, drained
- 1 medium potato, cooked
- 2 tbsp celery, finely chopped
- Salt, to taste
- 1 cup breadcrumbs
- 1 free-range egg

Method:
1. Start by warming the olive oil in a skillet and adding the onion, chili and ginger. Cook gently until sort. Then add the tuna to the pan and cook until the pan becomes dry.
2. Remove these ingredients from the pan. You can pop it into the fridge to help this along.
3. Next mash the potato and add to the tuna mix along with the celery and a pinch of extra salt.
4. Meanwhile, spread the breadcrumbs on a plate and break the egg into a medium bowl, whisking well.
5. Form into cutlets using your hands and then dip into the egg, then the breadcrumbs then pop into your air fryer.
6. Cook for 5-10 minutes on 350°F/ 180°C, turning halfway through.
7. Serve and enjoy!

Vegan & Vegetarian

Crispy Air Fried Tofu

There's nothing like fried tofu for giving you that satisfying chewy texture with a lightly crispy coating. It's perfect for throwing into a healthy salad, adding to a main meal or even for slicing and placing into sandwiches. Enjoy!

Serves: 4

Ingredients:
- 2 tbsp soy sauce
- 1 tsp rice vinegar
- 2 tsp toasted sesame oil (can use olive oil instead but it won't be so good!)
- 1 block firm tofu, pressed and cut into 1" (2cm) cubes
- 1 tbsp cornstarch

Method:
1. Start by grabbing a medium bowl and placing the marinade ingredients inside. Stir well to combine.
2. Next add the tofu chunks and leave to marinade for around 30 minutes to get tasty!
3. Then remove from the marinade and place onto a plate, along with the cornstarch. Toss well to coat, then transfer to your air fryer.
4. Cook on 370°F/190°C for 20 minutes.
5. Serve and enjoy!

Red Bean-Chipotle Burgers

Whenever you want an incredibly tasty vegan meal, hop into your kitchen to create these spicy, satisfying burgers. Containing a bunch of healthy protein, iron, and other great nutrients, they made a perfect meat substitute for anyone who doesn't want to eat meat.

Serves: 6

Ingredients:

- 16 oz. (450g) can kidney beans
- 1 small onion, peeled and cut into quarters
- 1 clove garlic
- ½ cup (45g) old fashioned oats (uncooked)
- ½ cup (125g) cooked brown rice
- 1-2 tsp chipotle chili powder
- 2 tbsp flour
- 1 tbsp tomato paste
- ½ tsp oregano
- ½ tsp thyme
- Salt and pepper, to taste

Method:

1. Start by opening up the tin of beans and wash them well under running water. Set to one side.
2. Now place the onion and garlic into your food processor and hit the whizz button until processed. Add the beans and then repeat. You want it to be finely chopped but not like a puree.
3. Add the rest of the ingredients, combine well, and put into the fridge to rest.
4. Now place some baking paper onto a baking sheet that will fit into your air fryer. Shape the burger mix into six and cook for 15-20 minutes on 390°F/200°C. Turn halfway through to cook properly.
5. Serve and enjoy!

Savory Lentil and Mushroom Burgers

The combination of lentils and mushrooms really hits the spot if you're a recent vegetarian or vegan, or want to experience a plant-based depth of flavor and nutrients. Mushrooms are a wonderful source of minerals and the added spices really make an incredible difference. Feel free to play with the flavors with this one- I love to make a light Mediterranean version by adding sundried tomatoes and fresh basil.

Serves: 3-6

Ingredients:
- 2 cups (150g) cooked lentils
- 2 tsp chia seeds
- 3 tbsp warm water
- 1 medium onion
- 6 oz. (170g) mushrooms, washed
- 3 cloves garlic
- 1/3 cup (46g) old fashioned oats
- 2 tbsp cornstarch
- 1 tbsp soy sauce
- 1 tbsp tomato paste
- ½ tsp dried oregano
- ½ tsp dried basil
- ½ tsp smoked paprika
- ¼ tsp dried thyme
- Salt and pepper, to taste

Method:
1. Start by giving your lentils a nice wash under running water, then set aside.
2. Also take a small bowl, add the chia seeds and warm water and pop to one side to thicken.
3. Chop the onions, mushrooms and garlic. Cook the onions and garlic in a skillet with a small amount of oil. Add the mushroom and continue to cook. Add a drop of water if needed.
4. Now transfer everything to the food processor with the lentils and pulse until combined.

5. Add the chia seeds and the other ingredients and pulse again to combine. Add more oats if it's too wet.
6. Pop into the fridge for 15 minutes to rest.
7. Now place some baking paper onto a baking sheet that will fit into your air fryer. Shape the burger mix into six and cook for 15-20 minutes on 390°F/200°C. Turn halfway through to cook properly.
8. Serve and enjoy!

Crispy Black-Eyed Peas

Just three words for these peas...yum, yum and yum! They're a beautiful snack, they're easy to make and they'll disappear faster than you'll believe!

Serve: 6

Ingredients:
- 15 oz. (425g) can black-eyed peas
- ½ tsp chili powder
- ¼ tsp salt optional
- 1/8 tsp chipotle chili powder
- 1/8 tsp black pepper

Method:
1. Firstly, open up the beans and rinse well under running water, then place to one side.
2. Now take a large bowl and mix together all the spices until well combined.
3. Add the peas to the spices and mix well to coat.
4. Place the peas into the wire basket of your air fryer and cook for 5-10 minutes on 360°F/180°C until crunchy.
5. Serve and enjoy!

Tempeh Bacon Lettuce and Tomato Sandwiches

You could enjoy these for breakfast, you could tuck in for snacks, you could eat them for dinner- they're THAT good. Enjoy!

Serves: 4

Ingredients:

- 8 oz. (225g) package tempeh
- 1 cup (235ml) warm vegetable broth
- 2-3 tbsp soy sauce
- 1 tsp Liquid Smoke
- 1/2 tsp onion powder
- 1/2 tsp garlic powder
- 1/4 tsp chipotle chili powder or smoked Spanish paprika
- Tomato slices and lettuce, to serve

Method:

1. Start by opening up the packet of tempeh and slice into pieces about ¼ inch (1/2 cm) thick.
2. Grab a medium bowl and add the remaining ingredients (apart from the tomato and lettuce). Stir well to combine.
3. Now place the slices of tempeh onto a baking tray (that fits into your air fryer) and pour over the flavor mix.
4. Pop into the air fryer and cook for 3-5 minutes on 360°F/ 180°C.
5. Remove from air fryer and place onto sliced bread with the tomato slices, the lettuce and any extra toppings you want. I can never resist a good dash of chili sauce.

Cauliflower Cheese Tater Tots

Tater tots are yummy, cheesy nuggets which are full of flavor and soo moreish. This version uses cauliflower instead of the usual potato and fresh chives to add a cauliflower cheese edge that is simply brilliant! Enjoy.

Serves: 12

Ingredients:
- 2 lbs. (910g) cauliflower
- 1 tbsp desiccated coconut
- 1 tbsp old-fashioned Oats
- 1 cup (90g) breadcrumbs
- 1 free-range egg
- Salt & Pepper
- 1 tsp garlic puree
- 2/3 cups (100g) onion, peeled and diced
- 1 tsp parsley
- 1 tsp chives
- 1 tsp oregano
- 1 ½ cups (150g) cheddar cheese, grated

Method:
1. Start by chopping the cauliflower into small pieces and then steaming it until soft. You can also use leftover cauliflower from another meal.
2. Meanwhile, take large bowl and add the coconut, oats and breadcrumbs, then stir well to combine.
3. Now take a small bowl, add the egg and whisk well to combine.
4. When the cauliflower is cooked, place it into the food processor with the salt, pepper and garlic puree. Hit that blend button until finely chopped, then pop into a clean tea towel and squeeze out the juice.
5. Place the dry cauliflower into a bowl with the onion, herbs and cheese, and mix well.
6. Form into tater tots, then dip into the egg, then the breadcrumbs.
7. Pop into your air fryer and cook for 15 minutes at 390°F/200°C.
8. Serve and enjoy!

Vegan Spicy Cream Cheese & Sundried Tomato Wrap

It's not that this delicious wrap is a flash of inspiration of anything out of the ordinary. It's just that most people never think of using their air fryer this way! Try this recipe as inspiration and then get it filled with whatever your heart desires! Lunchtime will never be the same.

Serves: 4

Ingredients:
- 4 flour tortilla wraps
- Vegan cream cheese
- Handful baby spinach
- Olives
- Sundried tomatoes, soaked
- Hot chili sauce, to taste

Method
1. Remove your tortilla wraps from the package and place flat on your work counter.
2. Now start with your fillings. Start with the cream cheese, then start layering with the rest of the ingredients. You can use your own judgment as to how much to add.
3. Carefully roll up into a wrap and place into your air fryer. Repeat with the remaining wraps. Cook at 300°F/150°C for 10 minutes.
4. Serve and enjoy (but be careful- the filling is likely to be very hot).

Vegetarian Lasagna

I wish someone had told me about vegetarian lasagna in the air fryer before! Because as we know, the regular kind takes so much time and effort to make, but this one just slashes the time away so you can eat a delicious, hearty meal faster. You can either make your own béchamel sauce, or substitute with the store-bought kind to make it even faster.

Serves: 2

Ingredients:

For béchamel sauce:
- 1 cup (240ml) milk
- 1 bay leaf
- 1 tsp butter
- 2 tbsp flour
- ½ cup (15g) baby spinach, shredded

For the lasagna:
- 1 tsp olive oil
- ½ cup (150g) chopped onions
- ½ cup (90g) bell pepper, chopped
- ½ cup (100g) chopped tomatoes
- 1 tsp tomato puree
- 1 tsp mixed herbs
- Salt and pepper, to taste
- 1 package lasagna sheets
- 1 tbsp cheese, grated

Method:
1. Let's start by making the béchamel sauce (if you're not using store bought). Get a pan, add your milk and a bay leave and bring to the boil. Keep it boiling for 2-3 minutes. Now cover and leave to rest for 20 minutes. Remove the bay leaf.
2. Now take a separate pan and gently melt the butter, then immediate add the flour and keep mixing to stop it getting lumpy.
3. Add the milk to the flour mixture and keep stirring, add salt and pepper and bring to the boil.

4. Turn down the heat and simmer until the sauce thickens, then turn off, add the chopped baby spinach and cover until you need to use it.
5. Now we can make the tomato sauce. Warm a small amount of oil in a skillet and add the onions. Cook for around 5 minutes, until soft. Then add the bell pepper and cook for a further 5 minutes.
6. Add the tomatoes, tomato puree, mixed herbs and salt and pepper and allow to simmer for just a minute or two to start the thickening process. You can take longer if you want a thicker sauce, but I like mine just barely done.
7. We can start layering now. Take a baking dish that will fit into your air fryer (or use the one provided) and great with oil. Then add some of the tomato sauce to the bottom, followed by the lasagna sheets, then the more sauce, then more lasagna, and finally top with the béchamel sauce and the grated cheese. Note- you can repeat the tomato-lasagna layers until they're all done.
8. Pop into your air fryer and cook for 15 minutes on 180°C/350°F.
9. Serve and enjoy!

Vegetable Spring Rolls

Mmmm...vegetable spring rolls that are golden, crispy and definitely not dripping with fat. They're healthy, they're light and they're perfect for a snack, lunch or part of a main meal. This is another recipe you can have fun with- play with the fillings and find what tastes best for you! Enjoy!

Serves: 2-4 (makes 10)

Ingredients:
- 1 tsp olive oil
- 1 green gonion, finely chopped
- 1 clove garlic, smashed
- 1 tsp ginger, minced
- ½ cup (25g) carrot, sliced
- ¼ yellow bell pepper, thinly sliced
- ¼ red bell pepper, thinly sliced
- 5-6 mushrooms, sliced
- ½ cup (50g) cabbage, sliced
- 1 tbsp vegetarian oyster sauce (optional)
- 1 tbsp soya sauce
- 2 birds eye chilis, finely chopped
- 10 spring roll sheets

To serve...
- 2 tbsp sweet chili sauce
- 2 tbsp soya sauce

Method:
1. Start by placing a small amount of oil into a skillet and gently fry the green onion, ginger and garlic until soft.
2. Add the carrot and cook for 5 minutes, until adding the rest of the veggies, except for the chili. Give it all a good stir to combine.
3. Stir through the oyster sauce and the soy sauce and keep cooking for 10-15 minutes until the pan is dry. Stir through the chili then leave to cool.
4. When the veggies are cool, take your spring roll sheets and place onto your work surface. Place a tablespoon of the mixture on top and start rolling. Repeat with all the rolls.
5. Now place into your air fryer and cook on 400°F/200°C for 10 minutes. Make sure you check halfway through and turn if needed.
6. Serve and enjoy!

Kale and Potato Nuggets

If you have some leftover potatoes, then these amazing nuggets will help you polish them off fast! They're simple, yummy and perfect for vegans and vegetarians. Packed with vital minerals and a ton of healthy vitamins, they'll leave you feeling stronger and raring to go!

Serves: 4

Ingredients:

- 2 cups (650g) finely chopped potatoes (raw or cooked)
- 1 tsp extra-virgin olive oil or canola oil
- 1 clove garlic, minced
- 4 cups (300g approx.) loosely packed coarsely chopped kale
- 1/8 cup almond milk
- ¼ tsp sea salt
- 1/8 tsp ground black pepper
- Vegetable oil spray, as needed

Method:

1. Start by cooking your potatoes in a large pan of boiling water. Drain and cool. Otherwise, you can use leftover potatoes.
2. Now warm a small amount of oil in a skillet and cook the garlic, followed by the kale. Cook for 2-3 minutes until it starts to soften, then pop into a large bowl.
3. Add the cooked potatoes to the bowl, followed by the milk, salt and pepper and mash well. Then throw in the kale and stir well to combine.
4. Shape into nuggets and cook at 390°F/ 200°C for 12-15 minutes.
5. Serve and enjoy!

Sweet Potato Dum Aloo

Imagine sinking your teeth into fluffy sweet potato coated in a gently spiced Indian-style tomato sauce gravy. Mmmm it's making me hungry just thinking about it! Make it tonight for dinner and I promise it will definitely become one of your go-to recipes. Enjoy!

Serves: 1-2

Ingredients:

- 2 cups (400g) sweet potatoes, scrubbed & cubed
- 1 tbsp olive oil
- 1 cup (150g) onions, sliced thinly
- 2 tsp Garam Masala
- 2 tbsp tomato paste
- 1 tbsp ginger - garlic Paste
- 2 tbsp vinegar
- 1 cup (235ml) water
- Salt, to taste
- 2 tbsp cilantro, chopped
- Oil spray

Method:

1. Start by chopping the sweet potato (if you haven't already done so), spray with oil and pop into your air fryer. Cook for 20 minutes at 200°C/ 400°F, turning midway through to cook evenly.
2. Meanwhile, place the olive oil into a skillet, place over a medium heat and cook the onion until brown.
3. Add the garam masala to the cooking onions, and stir for a minute until gently toasted. Follow with the tomato paste, ginger-garlic paste and cook for a minute or two.
4. Now add the vinegar and water and stir well. Cook over a low heat until simmers and thickens slightly.
5. When the sweet potatoes have cooked, remove them from the air fryer, toss through and sprinkle with the chopped coriander.
6. Serve and enjoy!

Stuffed Eggplant

Even if eggplants aren't your favorite veggie, I'm pretty sure that you'll adore these tender, Mediterranean treats. Eat them as they are, substitute the feta with whatever cheese you like, pimp them up with black olives and feel the flavor!

Serves: 4

Ingredients:

- 4 eggplants
- 1 tsp of salt and lemon juice
- 1 tbsp olive oil
- 1 chopped onion
- 2 cloves fresh garlic, minced
- 1 tomato, chopped
- Salt and pepper, to taste
- ½ bell pepper, chopped
- ½ tsp oregano
- ¼ cup feta cheese, chopped
- 1-2 tbsp tomato paste
- Coriander, chopped

Method

1. Start by chopping the top off the eggplant and removing most of the flesh from the center. Retain this flesh.
2. Pop into a bowl of water with salt or lemon juice to stop them browning as you do this, then dry and place in your air fryer for 3-4 minutes at 160°C/ 320°F.
3. Meanwhile, place the oil in a skillet and cook the onions and garlic until soft.
4. Add the tomato, salt, and eggplant flesh that you removed earlier. Cook until it gets soft.
5. Then add the bell pepper, oregano, feta, tomato paste, coriander and seasoning and mix nicely until combined.
6. Stuff this mixture into your eggplant 'shells' and pop into the air fryer. Cook on 350°F/180°C for 5 minutes, until perfectly cooked.
7. Serve and enjoy!

Chinese-Style Sticky Mushroom Rice

Sticky rice makes a lovely straightforward dinner that will light up your taste buds and keep your coming back for more. Serve it alone or even team it with bread, salad or even veggie burgers for a perfectly rounded meal.

Serves: 4-6

Ingredients:
- 16 oz. (450g) jasmine rice uncooked
- ½ cup (170ml) soy sauce
- 4 tbsp maple syrup
- 4 cloves garlic finely chopped
- 2 tsp Chinese 5-Spice
- ½ tsp ground ginger
- 4 tbsp vinegar
- 16 oz. (450g) cremini mushrooms
- ½ cup (75g) frozen peas

Method:
1. Start by cooking your rice! Place into a pan with approximately 5 cups water (you want a ratio of twice water to rice) and bring to the boil, covered. Cook for 6-10 minutes until the water is absorbed, then leave to rest with the lid on.
2. Meanwhile let's make the sauce. Start by mixing together the soy sauce, maple syrup, garlic, Chinese 5-Spice, ginger and vinegar in a bowl, then pop to one side.
3. Now cook your mushrooms by placing them into the air fryer and cooking for 10 minutes on 340°F/170°C.
4. Remove the mushroom from the air fryer, add the peas and pour over the sauce. Stir well to combine then return to the air fryer, cooking for 5 minutes.
5. Serve the mushrooms in sauce over the cooked rice and ENJOY!

Cakes and Desserts

Key Lime Cheesecake

I STILL find it amazing how such an amazing cheesecake can come straight from an air fryer- it's like magic. This one is exactly how a key lime cheesecake should be- it's tangy, sweet and you're going to love it!

Serves: 8

Ingredients:
- Some flour
- 6 digestive biscuits
- ¼ cup (50g) butter, melted
- 1 cup (250g) caster sugar
- 2 ¼ cups (500g) soft cheese
- 3 free-range eggs
- 1 tbsp honey
- 1 tbsp vanilla extract
- 6 fresh limes
- 2 tbsp Greek yogurt

Method:
1. Take a spring-form pan which will fit into your air fryer and rub the sides with flour.
2. Now crush the biscuits by hitting them with a rolling pin whilst still in their pan.
3. Melt the butter, then pour into a medium bowl. Add the biscuit crumbs and mix well until combined. Press this mixture into the bottom of your pre-prepared pan and set to one side.
4. Rub flour into the sides and the bottom of a spring form pan so that it becomes non-stick.
5. Now place the sugar and soft cheese into a large bowl and mix well with a hand mixer until well combined and thickened.
6. Then add the eggs, honey and vanilla and keep mixing, followed by the juice and grated rind of the limes plus the yogurt. Mix well to combine.
7. Pour the wet mixtures over the biscuit base and smooth the top so it looks pretty.
8. Pop into the air fryer and cook for 15 minutes on 350°F/180°C. Turn the heat down to 320°F/160°C and cook for another 10 minutes. Then turn down again and cook for 15 minutes on 300°F/150°C. Watch carefully- if you're using a smaller pan you might need to adjust the times.
9. Pop into the fridge for 6 hours until set. Serve and enjoy.

Chocolate Chip Cookies

These chocolate chip cookies really turn into something special when you cook them in an air fryer. They simply melt-in-your-mouth quite literally. Yummy!!

Serves: 10

Ingredients:
- ½ cup (100g) butter
- 1/3 cup (65g) brown sugar
- 1 cup cream
- 2 tbsp honey
- 1 ½ cups (180g) self-raising flour
- 3 ½ oz. (100g) chocolate, chopped into small pieces
- 1 tbsp milk

Method:
1. Start by preheating your air fryer to 350°F/180°C.
2. Now take a large bowl, add the butter and beat until soft.
3. Next add the sugar and cream and mix together until it gets light and fluffy!
4. Stir through the honey, followed by the flour and give it a mix until well combined, followed by the chocolate chunks (yum!) and the milk.
5. Take a greased baking sheet (which fits into your air fryer) and cook at 350°F/180°C for 8 minutes. Then turn down to 320°F/160°C and cook for 2 minutes or so until cooked in the middle.
6. Serve and enjoy! (trying not to eat them all at once!)

Strawberry Cupcakes with Creamy Strawberry Frosting

Want to impress your friends? Then give them these beautiful strawberry cupcakes. They look fantastic, they taste even better, and you're bound to have lots of fun licking the bowl when you've finished making them. If you have kids, you can even get them to help you out. For extra presentation points, serve topped with an extra slice of fresh strawberry and perhaps even a small mint leaf.

Serves: 10

Ingredients:

For the cupcakes:
- ½ cup (100g) butter
- ½ cup (100g) caster sugar
- 1 cup cream
- ½ tsp vanilla extract
- 2 free-range eggs
- 1 cup (110g) self-raising flour

For the frosting:
- ¼ cup (50g) butter
- ½ cup (100g) powdered sugar
- ½ tsp pink food coloring
- 1 tbsp cream, whipped
- ¼ cup (100g) fresh strawberries, blended

Method:

1. Start by warming your air fryer to 340F/170C.
2. Meanwhile, grab a large bowl and add the butter and sugar and cream together until soft, light and fluffy.
3. Next stir through the vanilla and the eggs and fold through until combined.
4. Add the flour and stir well until it's all mixed well.
5. Prepare a bun case (that will fit into the air fryer) and place a small amount of the batter into each. Make sure you leave a bit of a gap at the top as the cakes will rise as they cook.
6. Pop them into the air fryer and cook for 8 minutes. Remove when cooked and allow it to cool.
7. Let's make the topping. Start by creaming the butter and the icing sugar together until light, fluffy and creamy. Then add a few drops of food coloring and stir well.
8. Add the whipped cream and strawberry puree and mix well to combine.
9. Pipe the mixture onto your cooled cakes, then serve and enjoy!

Amazing Iced Donuts with Chocolate Icing

I always seem to suffer donut cravings whenever I'm far away from any stores and too tired to do anything about it. But it turns out that I can just use the power of my air fryer and create the fluffiest, most amazing donuts the world has ever seen.

Serves: 4

Ingredients:
For the donuts:
- 2 ½ tbsp butter
- ¼ cup (50g) caster sugar
- ¼ cup (50g) brown sugar
- 1 free-range egg
- ½ cup (118ml) milk
- 1 ½ cups (225g) self-raising flour
- 1 tsp baking powder

For the chocolate icing:
- ¼ cup (50g) butter
- ½ cup (100g) icing sugar
- ½ tsp brown food coloring
- 1 tsp whipped cream
- ½ tsp chocolate essence

Method:
1. Start by preheating the air fryer to 350°F/180°C, then turn your attention to making the donuts!
2. Start by grabbing a medium bowl and add together the butter and both sugars until light and lovely.
3. Then add the egg and the milk and mix well to combine.
4. Finally, stir through the flour and baking power, trying not to destroy the air from your mixture.
5. Form into donut shapes and push your finger through the middle until they look just like donuts.
6. Now pop onto a greased baking sheet (that will fit into your air fryer) and cook for 15 minutes until firm. Leave to cool for at least five minutes. Then let's make the icing.
7. Start by creaming the butter and the sugar together until it's wonderfully creamy. Then add the food coloring, cream, chocolate flavor and stir well to combine.
8. Pour icing over the top of the donuts and enjoy!

Fruit Crumble Mug Cakes

Fruit crumble is another of those recipes that just make me think of home! But until I tried this recipe, I'd never made a mug cake before. Now I'm a convert!! Try it for yourself and you'll see just how tasty and fast they can be. You can use whatever fruit you want to for this recipe, especially if it's in season. I LOVE apples and blackberries!

Serves: 4

Ingredients:
- 3 tbsp old-fashioned oats
- 4 plums
- 1 small apple
- 1 small pear
- 1 small peach
- Handful blueberries
- 3 tbsp brown sugar
- 1 tbsp honey
- ½ cup (110g) plain flour
- ¼ cup (50g) butter

Method:
1. Start by preheating your air fryer to 320°F/160°C, then start to prepare your fruit. Depending on the fruit you choose, this might involve removing the cores or stones, washing or removing any skin. Dice into small pieces.
2. Now place some of each of the fruit into the bottom of four mugs. Then cover with the brown sugar and honey until covered. Place to one side.
3. Then we need to make the topping. Grab a bit bowl and place the flour and butter into a bowl. Rub the butter into the flour until it looks like breadcrumbs, then stir through the flour. Mix well to combine.
4. Put this mixture on top of your fruit crumble and then cook in the air fryer for 10 minutes. Then turn up the heat to 400°F/200°C and cook for another 5 minutes.
5. Serve and enjoy! Tastes wonderful with ice cream or custard!

Chocolate Profiteroles

I have to admit that profiteroles are by far my most favorite desert in the world! And this recipe really doesn't disappoint! Because who wouldn't love fresh, cream-filled profiteroles drizzled with luscious chocolate sauce. Mmmm....

Serves: 9

Ingredients:
For the profiteroles:
- 1 ¼ cup (300ml) water
- ½ cup (100g) butter
- 1 cup (200g) plain flour
- 6 free-range eggs

For the cream filling:
- 2 tsp vanilla extract
- 2 tsp powdered sugar
- 1 ¼ cup (300ml) whipped cream

For the chocolate sauce:
- 3 ½ oz. (100g) milk chocolate, chopped
- ¼ cup (50g) butter
- 2 tbsp whipped cream

Method:
1. Start by preheating the air fryer to 340°F/170°C. Then let's make those profiteroles.
2. Place the water into a large pan, add the butter and bring the water to the boil.
3. Remove the pan from the heat then start gently stirring in the flour. Don't rush this part as it could go lumpy!
4. Then pop it back onto the heat until dough forms. Set to one side until it cools. Make sure you do this bit properly.
5. Now add the eggs and mix well until you have smooth dough. Form into profiterole shapes then place into the basket of your air fryer and cook for 10 minutes on 350F/180C.
6. Meanwhile, make the cream filling by whisking all the cream ingredients together. Set to one side.
7. Now make the chocolate topping by melting the chocolate, butter and cream together in a Bain Marie and mixing as it melts. Keep mixing until it goes shiny and delicious looking.
8. When the profiteroles are cooked, slice open and fill with the cream mixture, then top with the chocolate sauce.
9. Serve and enjoy!

Easy Chunky Chocolate Muffins

There's nothing like the smell of freshly cooked chocolate muffins wafting around your kitchen, and let's face it- who can really resist?? This recipe makes twelve delicious muffins, bursting with chunky chocolate pieces and dripping flavor. Amazing! Make them!

Serves: 12

Ingredients:
- 1 cup (200g) self-raising flour
- 1 cup (225g) caster sugar
- 2 tbsp (25g) cocoa powder
- ½ cup (100g) butter
- 2 free-range eggs
- 5 tbsp milk
- ½ tsp vanilla extract
- Water
- 3 oz. (85g) milk chocolate, chopped into large chunks

Method:
1. Start by preheating your air fryer to 350F/180C.
2. Now take a large bowl and add the flour, sugar and cocoa and give it all a nice mix until well combined.
3. Rub in the butter until it starts looking like breadcrumbs. Then add the eggs, milk and vanilla and mix well to combine. Add some water or a drop of milk to thin.
4. Then we can think about the chocolate. Break or chop into medium pieces then throw this into the batter and mix well.
5. Spoon into pre-prepared bun cases (which fit into the air fryer) and cook for 9 minutes on 350°F/180°C then turn it down to 320°F/160°C and cook for 6 minutes.
6. Serve warm if you can.

Cinnamon Rolls

Whenever it comes to making great bread or bread-dough based treats, far too many people think that it's just too hard and they'll never get it right. But they couldn't be more wrong. Buy the frozen dough and you'll simply need to shape, leave to rise and then cook. Perfect, if you ask me!

Serves: 8

Ingredients:

For the cinnamon rolls:
- 1 lb (450g) bread dough, thawed
- ¼ cup (100g) butter, melted and cooled
- ¾ cup (165g) brown sugar
- 1 ½ tbsp ground cinnamon

For the cream cheese glaze:
- 4 oz. (115g) cream cheese, softened
- 2 tbsp butter, softened
- 1 ¼ cups (155g) powdered sugar
- ½ tsp vanilla

Method:

1. Make sure your bread dough is at room temperature, then roll into a large rectangle 13"x 11" (approx. 30cm x 26cm). Place the long side closest to you, then brush the whole thing with melted butter, leaving a margin along the side furthest away from you.
2. Take a medium bowl and combine the sugar and the cinnamon, then sprinkle over the dough.
3. Roll up lengthways and seal at the uncovered edge, then cut into eight pieces. Leave to rise for 1-2 hours.
4. Meanwhile make the glaze by placing the cream cheese and butter into a pan and melting over a low heat. Combine well then add the powdered sugar and vanilla, and keep stirring until smooth.
5. Check your rolls- if they have risen and are almost double their original size, you can preheat your air fryer to 350°F/ 180°C.
6. Place four rolls into the fryer and cook for 10 minutes, turning halfway through. Repeat with the other rolls.
7. Allow to it cool then cover with the glaze.
8. Serve and enjoy!

Mini Apple Pies

These tiny apple pies are absolutely gorgeous. They're perfect for any time, whether that's a party, a friendly gathering, something lovely for dessert or simply a well-deserved snack, and they taste beautiful.

Serves: 9

Ingredients:
- ¾ cup (75g) plain flour
- 2 tbsp (30g) butter
- 3 ¼ tsp caster sugar (plus a pinch extra)
- Cold water
- 2 medium red apples
- Pinch cinnamon

Method:
1. Start by preheating your air fryer to 350°F/180°C.
2. First, we'll be making the pastry. Grab a large bowl and add the flour and butter. Rub in until it starts looking like breadcrumbs. Add the sugar and stir well to combine. Then add the water and form into dough.
3. Find baking tins that will fit into your air fryer and grease them well. Roll out the pastry and place into the tins.
4. Let's turn to the fruit. Simply peel and dice the apples and place into the tin, topped with a pinch of cinnamon and a pinch of sugar.
5. Top with a pastry lid and prick with a fork to allow the steam to escape.
6. Cook for 18 minutes, then allow to cool slightly before serving.

Chocolate Marble Cake

I LOVE the way this chocolate marble cake looks and smells when it's straight out of the oven- I just can't resist cutting myself a big chunk and tucking right in! As ever, it's easy to make, ready fast and even a kid can make it.

Serves: 6-8

Ingredients:
- 2/3 cup (150g) salted butter, melted
- 1 tbsp cocoa powder
- ½ cup (100g) caster sugar
- 3 free-range eggs
- 1 cup (110g) self-raising flour, sieved
- 1/2 tsp lemon juice

Method:
1. Start by preheating your air fryer to 180, and greasing and lining a round pan which fits into your air fryer. I like to use one that's 5"/12cm.
2. Now grab a large bowl and add 3 tablespoons on the melted butter and cocoa powder, then mix until it forms a paste. Set aside.
3. Taking another bowl, beat the remaining butter with the sugar until it's light and creamy. Add the eggs and mix well, followed by the flour, and stir until smooth. Finally add the lemon juice and stir again.
4. Pour into the pre-prepared tin. Then gently pour the cocoa mixture over the top, moving around as you pour. Use a knife to swirl it around in the tin.
5. Pop into the air fryer for 15 minutes. Test the center with a skewer and return to the air fryer for a minute or two if not properly cooked.
6. Cook in pan and enjoy!

Apple Cinnamon Latkes

Latkes are traditionally served at Hanukkah- the Jewish festival of lights and are made from combining potatoes with eggs to make a delicious treat, but this apple-cinnamon variety takes it to a whole new level.

Serves: 6-8

Ingredients:
- 2 Granny Smith apples, peeled & quartered
- ½ tsp cinnamon
- 1 tbsp caster sugar
- 2 lbs (900g) baking potatoes, peeled & quartered
- 1 shallot, grated
- 2 free-range eggs, beaten
- ½ cup (65g) flour
- 1 tsp salt

Method:
1. Start by grating your apples in a food processor and placing them into a bowl with the cinnamon and sugar.
2. Grate the potatoes and the shallot and add those to the bowl too. Stir well to combine.
3. Now throw in your beaten eggs and mix well to combine again, followed by the flour and salt and stir again.
4. Form into patties and place onto a non-stick baking tray which fits into your air fryer.
5. Cook on 360°F/180°C for 10 minutes. Make sure you check them and flip mid-way through cooking.
6. Serve and enjoy!

Banana and Raisin Bread

Banana bread is amazing on its own, but the addition of a handful or two of raisins gives it an extra injection of sweetness, chewiness and even nutrition. Play with the quantities of raisins you add, and why not even think about throwing in your own extras like sunflower seeds, chia seeds or chopped fruit?

Serves: 8

Ingredients:
- ¼ cup (50g) butter, at room temperature
- 1/3 cup (65g) brown sugar
- 1 free-range egg
- 1 banana, mashed
- 2 tbsp honey
- 1 tbsp raisins
- 1 cup (110g) self-raising flour
- ½ tsp cinnamon
- Pinch salt, to taste

Method:
1. Start by preheating your air fryer to 320°F/160°C and greasing a ring tin. Make sure it fits inside your air fryer.
2. Now take a large bowl and mix together the butter and sugar until light and creamy.
3. Add the egg, banana and honey and beat well until it's all combined well.
4. Throw in the raisins, flour, cinnamon and a pinch of salt and then mix to make a cake batter.
5. Pop into the air fryer and cook for 30 minutes.
6. Check to see if it's cooked in the middle by inserting a skewer in the middle. If not, return to the air fryer for another five minutes and check again.
7. Cook in the tin and then serve and enjoy!

Peanut Butter Banana Dessert Bites

These are a very special treat that you will definitely want to try very VERY soon. They're very simple to make and taste heavenly when served with cream or icecream.

Serves: 12

Ingredients:
For the bites:
- 1 large banana
- 12 Won Ton wrappers
- ½ cup peanut butter
- 1-2 tsp oil

For the extras:
- Chocolate chips
- Raisins
- M&Ms
- Ground cinnamon or ginger

Method:
1. Start by preheating your air fryer to 380°F/190°C.
2. Slice the banana into rounds and put into bowl of water so it doesn't brown.
3. Lay out the Won Ton wrappers on your counter, and place a slice of banana and a teaspoon of peanut butter onto each piece. You can also add any of the extras you like.
4. Now brush the edges with water and bring the corners of the Won Ton Wrapper into the middle.
5. Pop into your air fryer, spray with oil and cook for 6 minutes.
6. Serve and enjoy!

Vegan Apple and Blueberry Crumble

Vegans have a sweet tooth too! And they're definitely going to enjoy this delicious apple and blueberry crumble. Just the thought of it is making me drool!

Serves: 4

Ingredients:
- ½ cup (50g) frozen blueberries
- 1 medium apple, finely diced
- ¼ cup (40g) brown rice flour
- 2 tbsp sugar
- ½ tsp ground cinnamon
- 2 tbsp non-dairy butter

Method:
1. Start by preheating your air fryer to 350°F/175°C and find and ovenproof baking pan or ramekin.
2. Pop the blueberries and apples into the pan and set aside.
3. Now take a small bowl and add the flour, sugar, cinnamon and butter. Mix well to combine and then pop over the top of the fruit.
4. Cook for 12 minutes, then allow to cool slightly before serving.
5. Enjoy!

Final words...

Congratulations! You've come with me right to the very end of comprehensive air fryer book into which we've packed over a hundred mouth-watering, easy and inspiring recipes that you can recreate with the help of that wonderful, healthy piece of kitchen technology- your air fryer.

As we mentioned in the introduction, air fryer is a wonderful tool as you can enjoy the same crunchy, cooked, indulgent flavor of all your favorite foods, but with just a fraction of the calories and unhealthy fat contents. That's right- you're now armed with everything you need to eat healthy and still enjoy your food to the max. If you ask me, that's a truly wonderful thing!

So please, don't let your air fryer be just another of those purchases that seems like a good idea at the time, but just lies there in a box in the pantry. Actually use it! Make the most of your air fryer by whipping up these amazing recipes. And when you've done that, you should have the confidence to start recreating all your favorite meals with less mess, less fuss and fat fewer unhealthy fat calories.

Have fun!

Before I go...

Just wanted to say a quick thank you for grabbing this book- I've had so much fun collecting my favorite recipes for you, and I must admit, I couldn't resist cooking up everything I've share in the deserts section just one more time...you know, for research's sake...

If you like what you've read, please do share your thoughts by **leaving a review on Amazon**. It only takes a few minutes for you, but it makes a world of difference for me. Many thanks!

Made in the USA
San Bernardino, CA
28 December 2017